Bond
Bubble
Burst

국채버블
대붕괴

:채권투자로 부자되는 비밀

The fall of wealth and jackpot chance of wealth

Copyright Notice

Bond
Bubble
Burst

국채버블
대붕괴
:채권투자로 부자되는 비밀
The fall of wealth and jackpot chance of wealth

Copyright(c)2024 by Sohn DaeShig.All right reserved.
Published by Sohn DaeShig,

Contact Information: sohn2738@naver.com

About the author:

The author was born in 1952. He was born during the Korean War and experienced all of Korea's political, economic, social, and cultural developments from the 1960s, when Korea was at its most difficult, to the present day, when it is one of the poorest countries on earth. He has been studying and investing in stocks and apartments for over 50 years.

After retiring from KBS as a PD specializing in current affairs for 30 years, in September 2011, he started writing financial technology (fintech) books professionally by gathering his investment experience and research materials in his spare time. So far, he has written 10 books on financial technology, obtained a real estate broker license, and completed a graduate CRO course.

Bibliographies: These're only author Sohn DaeShig's main books

1) Jan.2,2018.(A financial secret handbook that only passes on to children,390 pages) Korean Edition

2) Apr.2,2018.(Tears of the Japanese,261pages) Korean Edition

3) Mar.22,2019.(Rent investors are stupid investors,371pages) Korean Edition

4) Aug. 2019: Tears of Korean: How salaried and poor people get rich, a story you'll only want to tell your children

5) Aug.10,2021.(The Fall of Riches,298pages) Korean Edition

6) Dec.1,2021.(Tears of Korea,424pages) Korean Edition. Korea, like Japan, will run out of money to invest: Short Term, Long Term Deflation War. Big Cycle cyclical investing is the answer!

7) Sep. 1, 2023(Wealth Creation, The Hidden Story,499pages)(How to start investing at age 60 and succeed) Korean Edition

8) March 4,2024 (Dollar Swap Fintech Make 800% .Assets Market Rotation

investing Formula.Pentagon Investing Method, 374pages) Korean & English Edition

(9)June,2024 : Why Gold? No Bitcoin! : Bitcoin goes to $0 as bubble bursts.

(10)July.2024:Bond Bubble Burst: The fall of wealth and jackpot chance of wealth

Prologue

– 5 –

The book is titled The Great Collapse of the Government Bond Bubble: Secrets to Getting Rich in Bonds.

Most people would look at the title of the book and think, "The Great Collapse of the Government Bond Bubble," when there hasn't been a boom in government bonds yet, and therefore no bubble, and think it's getting ahead of itself.

However, I think Korea is starting to see a sovereign bond investment boom with the sale of government bonds for private investment exclusively.

After that, the rest of the world will see a massive surge in government bonds as longterm deflation begins in earnest. This is also a huge bubble-generating factor.

Although the book is titled "The Great Collapse of the Government Bond Bubble: The Secrets to Getting Rich in Bonds," the Great Collapse of all bonds, including government bonds, will happen soon, and the collapse of all assets will happen soon. That's why it's called the Great Collapse.

I emphasized the word "Great Collapse" because it is a long term deflation that started in 2016, and the collapse of all goods will begin at least until 2029 in Korea and 2048 in the world.

However, bonds, such as government bonds of all countries, are due for a big bounce right after the collapse, i.e., as soon as foreigners stop selling to avoid currency losses. However, the secondary bubble bursting of government bonds and other bonds due to a secondary interest rate hike will first appear, and then the big bull run will begin.

During a long term deflation, that is, in the case of Japan, bubbles accumulate in government bonds for 32 years, which is the situation in Japan today, and this is when the largest bubble in history is created in government bonds and other bonds. This fact is the most important.

When the FED raises interest rates for the second time to fight secondary inflation, the world sees a massive collapse in all assets.

Panicked foreign investors dump all foreign assets. As foreigners sell to avoid currency exchange losses due to the surge in the dollar's exchange rate, all bonds and government bonds begin a temporary crash.

This process of crashing and soaring is impossible to survive or deal with if the outcome is not predicted in advance. Therefore, this book provides readers with the opportunity to rehearse what is to come, and introduces the secret to getting rich from investing in bonds, or government bonds, in advance. In the U.S., all of these situations are put on banks and tested in advance. It's called stress testing.

I've written a lot of financial books over the years, and while I always focus on the present, I usually try to predict what will happen in two or three years, using all my experience and knowledge.

I often write warnings that if you don't invest now because the future is predicted to change in this way, you will lose a lot of money.

Since the world, including Korea, has already entered a long term deflation in 2016, I analyze the Japanese economy, which has been in a long term deflation since December 1988, and use it as a basis for my articles. Japan is now out of long term deflation in 2020, 32 years after the last long term deflation, thanks to Abenomics.

If I compare the results of the predictions and the books that have already been published, we can see that this time in Korea, the cycle ended in June 2021, just as the authors claimed, and the stock market ended in June 2021, and the apartment market began a major decline in December 2021, six months later.

The author's books, Tears of a Korean, The Secret Handbook of Finance, and others, which warned readers not to join KIKO or ELS, proved to be correct.

What is predicted in the future is the great collapse of the sovereign debt bubble: the secret to getting rich investing in bonds and the ghost dollarization of overseas investment funds, which means that no one should invest overseas.

The sharp increase in interest rates in the U.S. has already significantly deflated the bubble in all bonds, including U.S. government bonds, and the valuation of government bonds has collapsed by about 50%.

However, there is already a moderate bubble in bonds, as people rushed to invest in bonds in anticipation of a future rate cut.

Even now, the rush to government bonds continues, which means that the bubble in bonds, including government bonds, is getting bigger and bigger.

In this book, you will learn the general theory of the bond

market, as well as the upcoming collapse and creation of bond bubbles. You will learn how to make money and how to survive in such a situation.

Contrary to popular belief, inflation rates below 3% will not be reached in the next 4-5 years and certainly not in the next decade. For higher for longer is a reality.

For those who are already invested in bonds and those who are going to get caught up in the bubble and invest in bonds, especially government bonds, I predict that they will experience a momentary bursting of the bond bubble and a long period of bond bubbles.

In other words, the bond market will experience one crash and a long bull run. Right now, the world is in a long period of deflation. On one side, inflation is underway. It's a confusing state.

No one should forget that the first long deflation in human history, the Great Depression in the US, lasted 19 years, and the long deflation in Japan lasted 32 years (2020-1988=32).

As the author will explain in detail later, after the secondary bubble burst, government bonds are the only bonds with a jackpot chance. With such a long term deflation, we could be in for a whopping 30 years of profits.

Even in the 1980s in the US, the annualized return on US government bonds was a whopping 18.9%. You could have been enjoyed this return for 30 years. That is, if you bought US government bonds then.

This is what happened when Paul Volcker failed to fight 12.1% inflation. It's normal to not be able to control inflation in the short term. If 9.1% inflation is what Powell can control with a 5.25% FED funds rate, what's to worry about?

I don't think Powell will be able to catch inflation like Paul Volcker did this time. Using a simple proportional equation, the maximum expected rate is a whopping 18.7%. History has shown that the first rate hike is never enough to control inflation. Like Volcker's so-called mistake, Powell's is a foregone conclusion.

In fact, until now, most investors didn't even know what bonds, especially government bonds, were, and they were right not to invest in them.

Even if you work in a securities company or a banking or financial company, bonds are an asset that most of them are not even familiar with.

Until now,government bonds have been the exclusive goods that treat only in departments of brokerage main houses.
But now, in the age of bond popularization, everyone needs to know.

In addition, according to the new asset cycle investment method, or Pentagon investment method, which the author has just established, everyone must go through the bond investment process once every 10 years when making a financial investment.

Therefore, this book's method of investing in government bonds is a general theory of bond investment during a general recession, and it is a basic principle of bond investment that should always be remembered and practiced.

In particular, this book also analyzes how to invest in government bonds during the long term deflation that began in 2016.

In other words, this book summarizes both ordinary

government bonds and government bonds during a long term deflation.

In other words, this book summarizes the secrets of investing in government bonds in the event of a government bond bubble burst.

2024.6.
Pangyo in Korea

Table of Contents

Prologue 5

Chapter 1) Types of bonds and an overview..............13
Chapter 2) The time has come to mass market bonds...........17
Chapter 3) Why government bond bubbles happen...................30
Chapter 4) Government Bond Bubbles and Modern Monetary Theory...43
Chapter 5) Only invest in government bonds..........................47
Chapter 6) Another Limitation of Investing in Government Bonds.........55
Chapter 7) The government bond market freaking out over a quarter-point change in interest rates. Why?..................61

Chapter 8) How High Can Government Bonds Go?.................71
Chapter 9) Trading government bonds in the real market...........79
Chapter 10) Government bond market gains disappear like smoke at maturity..85
Chapter 11) The First Great Collapse of the Government Bond Bubble Has Already Passed....................................87
Chapter 12) Reasons for the collapse of the second government bond bubble: Scenarios ①②③.................................114
Chapter 13)How to Invest When the Government Bond Bubble Bursts...123
  1) Buy government bonds that foreigners are dumping.
  2) Buy an eligible inverse
  3) Buy stock in the Macquarie Infrastructure Fund.
  4)Gold and Bitcoin are not investments at all.
Chapter 14)The Ghost Dollar is Born....................128
Chapter 15) A concrete example of a jackpot during the bond bubble burst..131

(1) Reconstruction Ministry bonds and Vietnam, etc.
(2) There's a huge opportunity in North Korean government bonds.
(3) Success story of the founder of Mirae Asset Securities at the time of the IMF
(4)Hit the jackpot with BW
(5) Apartment bonds
Chapter 16)Secrets to Getting Rich Investing in Bonds (government bonds)..144
Chapter 17) Income Tax on Financial Investments and Investing in Government Bonds..158

Epilogue..161

Chapter 1) Types of bonds and an overview

When we trade money between individuals, we use something called iou(promissory note).
 It requires conditions, such as when the money will be paid back and at what rate of interest.

People give or take collateral, which is something of value, in case they can't pay back the money.
Sometimes there's no collateral, and people just credit each other. Or a person might vouch for you.

When people borrow money from a bank, they have to submit something called a loan document. This is also a borrowing certificate with a different name. Governments also need money for infrastructure and to improve the welfare of their citizens.

The government is required by law to spend money within the limit of the revenue (taxes) it collects from the people. If there is a shortage of money, they use borrowing certificates to borrow money from companies, individuals, or other countries.

When the government borrows money from companies or individuals, it can't just write out borrowing certificates. It would be unmanageable and undignified, so the borrowing certificates that governments issue when they borrow money are called government bonds.

Companies also need money to invest to make more money, and the bills they issue are called corporate bonds.

It's easy for people to think that the governments can just borrow from the central bank without issuing government bonds, but then no one can control the government and it will cause inflation or hyperinflation, etc. It needs parliamentary approval.

Therefore, if the government wants to spend more money than taxes, it has no choice but to issue government bonds (borrowing certificates). This is the essence of government bonds.

Bonds can be categorized into many different types depending on the situation. There are government and municipal bonds, coupon bonds, discount bonds, compounding bonds, guaranteed bonds, secured bonds, unguaranteed bonds, and so on. The types and names can be learned in other books, and we will summarize some of the key points in this book!

(1) It is important to distinguish between maturing bonds and perpetual bonds.
Until now, bonds have all been issued in maturing form, but recently, they have also been issued in perpetual form, which means that they can be paid off in perpetuity. Perpetual bonds are bonds that pay interest in perpetuity and have no maturity.

It is a new type of bond that has never existed before. Since they don't have to be paid back forever, they are also like capital stock.

Therefore, they are included in the capital account. That's why they are also called new capital securities.In

Korea, a few banks and companies have issued them.

The issue terms of the perpetual bonds of Swiss Credit Suisse, which were eliminated in the M&A, have been highlighted.

The perpetual bonds issued by the company were unilaterally canceled by the company in accordance with the contract, i.e., according to the terms of issue, without any compensation, and without paying any price.

It is legal because it was done in accordance with the provisions contained in the terms of issue. Not all perpetual bonds have the same issuance conditions, so you need to know all the issuance conditions for each perpetual bond before investing.
Under certain conditions, it is possible to burn the bond , decrease the capital, etc.

(2) It's also important to recognize the distinction between long term and short term bonds It is important to remember that this is not divided by the duration at the time of issuance, but by the remaining duration at the time of purchase or sale.

Even if you issued a 10 year bond, if it has a maturity of one year or less, it becomes a short term bond, which should be classified by the remaining time to maturity.

(3) Bond yield is the percentage of the principal amount of money earned by investing in a bond. From the lender's point of view, it is a profit, so the word bond yield is used. However, from the perspective of the borrower, it is the bond interest rate.

In the end, when it comes to bonds,(bond yield)(=bond revenue rate)(=interest rate). Don't get confused: government bonds and government bonds are the same thing.

Chapter 2) The time has come to mass market bonds

Everyone would be happy if they could just live on the rent that comes in easily every month, and life would always be fun. However, there is also a way to live more comfortably and safely than renting a house by earning interest on government bonds.

There are many types of bonds, including government bonds issued by the government, corporate bonds issued by companies, and municipal bonds issued by local governments, but the best bonds are government bonds (treasury bonds), which pay principal and interest until the country goes bankrupt. They are classified as risk-free assets because they are risk-free.

In other words, the best bonds are government bonds. However, they pay less interest than other bonds.
Since U.S. Treasuries are equal to the dollar and pay interest, governments often buy them as a way to store their foreign exchange reserves (dollars). Nowadays, it is fashionable to invest wealth overseas, so there are also domestic ant investors who buy US government bonds.

In Korea, securities companies also sell US government bonds as a product in the form of RPs. Currently, the interest rate on US government bonds is about 3%, so if you convert it to an annualized figure, an investment of 100 million won will earn about 3 million won per year in interest. After deducting 15.4% taxes, it is about 2.5 million won.

That's an average monthly income of 210,000 won. It is commonly said that a family of two needs 2.7 million won per month for minimum living expenses, so if you want to live only on interest from government bonds, you need to buy at least 1.2 billion won worth of government bonds to achieve a monthly income of 2.7 million won, depending on the exchange rate.

Few people have this much money in cash, and fewer people invest it like it's a dried up persimmon. The United States has a high debt-to-income ratio.

Unlike the U.S., Korea doesn't have a lot of debt, so there are not many government bonds issued, and there are not many different types of bonds such as 2-year, 5-year, 10-year, 20-year, and 30-year bonds.

Due to the low trading volume, the market price is not properly formed. Buying and selling can be done directly at the securities company or through HTS(Home Trading Syetem), but the trading volume is also small, so it is not easy to trade. Currently, the interest rate of 30-year government bonds in Korea is about 2%, which is lower than that of US government bonds.

In Korea, securities companies also sell US bonds as a product in the form of RPs. If the interest rate on U.S. government bonds is 3%, an annualized investment of 100 million won will earn about 300 million won in interest per year. After deducting 15.4% taxes, it is about 2.5 million won.

That's an average monthly income of 210,000 won. It is commonly said that a family of two needs 2.7 million won per month for minimum living expenses, so if you want to live only on interest from government bonds, you need to buy at least 1.2 billion won worth of government bonds to achieve a monthly income of 2.7 million won, depending on the exchange rate.

Few people have this much money in cash, and fewer people invest it like it's a dried up persimmon. The United States has a high debt-to-income ratio.

Unlike the U.S., Korea doesn't have a lot of debt, so there are not many government bonds issued, and there are not many different types of bonds such as 2-year, 5-year, 10-year, 20-year, and 30-year bonds.

Due to the low trading volume, the market price is not properly formed. Buying and selling can be done directly at the securities company or through HTS(Home Trading Syetem), but the trading volume is also small, so it is not easy to trade.

Currently, the 30-year government bond in Korea has an interest rate of around 2%, which is lower than the US government bond.

Government bonds are notoriously volatile during normal times. So in many ways, it's not a good fit for retail investors, which is to say that government bonds are not a good investment in normal times. However, there are times when you should buy government bonds and times when you should sell them.

That's when you're in stage 5 of the Pentagon Investing Method, and when you're in the midst of a long term deflation. Korea's deflation started in 2016 and is already in its eighth year. It's just that we're not feeling it yet, and while deflation is underway, mild inflation is also underway in Korea for a while due to quantitative easing by other countries.

According to the Pentagon Investing Method, which is analyzed and theorized by the author, in the last five stages of the asset market investment cycle, everyone should invest in government bonds to maximize profits. By the time you reach the last investment asset, government bonds, you will have already gained nearly eight times the return you made earlier.

This large sum of money would be invested entirely in government bonds, which would buy about 8 times as much government bonds as the money invested. The fifth stage of the Pentagon Investing Method is when the economy has already tipped and is about seven or eight years into a state of deflation.

It's no secret that cash is best at this point, but even then, investing in government bonds can add another 1-2x to your wealth. And an even better investment than cash is the Macquarie Infrastructure Fund.

Back to the point,
Government bonds are bonds issued by the government, so they're like cash. They pay interest every quarter, unless the government goes bankrupt. At maturity, you get 100% of your principal back. Usually, the interest rate is between 1% and 3%, but when interest rates rise, the price of bonds drops, and when they fall, they soar.

For a 10 year government bond, the price of the bond will rise and fall by about 7% (Decimals are truncated, hereafter always the same) as interest rates rise and fall by 1%.

I use the words " surge" and " crash" because the absolute amount of gains or losses is large, as all of the investments made according to the Pentagon's five-step investment method are rotated into government bonds. This is because the investment will have increased by about 8 times.

Also, a 1% fluctuation in interest rates can cause a 7% fluctuation in bond prices. This is because government bonds are an asset that rarely fluctuates in price during normal times, so it feels more like a crash or a surge.

There are many thick books on the market about investing in government and corporate bonds, but there is very little information to be gained from reading them. They don't tell you that if interest rates fall by 1%, the price of a 10-year bond will go up by about 7%, which is a key piece of information for bond investing.

The key information is that the 20 year bond will naturally rise 14% when interest rates fall by 1%, and the 30 year bond will jump 21%. The reverse is also true for proportional declines.

Therefore, this information is important and should never be forgotten by retail investors. The relationship between interest rates and bond yields is the same in any country and in any era. In fact, there are more books on bond investing that don't even disclose this information.

This information has been shared only with bond rating companies and institutional investors. In Korea, there are three or four companies specializing in bond rating, or credit rating.

* As deflation progresses, interest rates are destined to fall steadily as it progresses. Typically, government bonds are issued at 1 to 3% or less. In Korea, long deflation is expected to continue until around 2029, so the relative value of cash will continue to rise.

This doesn't mean that cash is actually going up, but rather that the purchasing power of cash is increasing because everything else in the world is decreasing in value, including real estate, stocks, necessities, gold, silver, and so on. That's why we say that cash is best in deflation, whether it's a short or long deflation.

Cash is said to be best even if it doesn't increase, meaning it earns little interest, while government bonds are better because they earn interest plus capital gains, or price appreciation. Like bonds, the Macquarie Infrastructure Fund's price fluctuates based on interest rates.

There are stocks and bonds in the securities market.The Korean securities market doesn't have a lot of trading volume and doesn't provide quotes, so you might ask, how can I buy government bonds?

Just in case (?), there are government bond ETFs listed on the stock market. Buying and selling through them has a similar effect to owning the actual bonds.

There are short-term government bond ETFs, 3-year government bond ETFs, 5-year government bond ETFs, 10-year government bond ETFs, 20-year government bond ETFs, and so on. Bond ETFs are not actually investments in bonds; they are investments in bond yields or bond futures.

Not long ago, Brazilian government bonds were popular in the market. They are completely tax-free and pay 10% interest. If the value of the Brazilian currency remained unchanged, a 10% annualized return on Brazilian government bonds would be the best investment. Compare that to the 2% interest rate on Korean CDs, and it's easy to see why.

However, it was an avoidable investment if you think, "If it is such a good investment, why would securities companies sell it to the public instead of investing their own funds and enjoying the profit until the bond matures? Securities firms pocketed a 3% upfront fee and sold trillions of dollars to gullible domestic investors.

The world of investing is a jungle.
Investing is a zero sum game. You can't trust anyone, you have to study, learn, and practice.

If you look internationally, there are many countries that have seen their government bond prices collapse ("government bond yields soar"), such as Argentina, Greece, and Turkey. And there is an international practice that if the yield on a country's government bonds reaches 6%, it is considered a country default. In other words, it becomes impossible for any country to get dollar financing from anyone at 6% interest.

These countries can only borrow dollars, the international currency, through IMF bailouts. This means that 6% is the highest interest rate on government bonds that is customary internationally. Overseas investments in government bonds in other countries are doomed, like Brazilian government bonds, if the exchange rate between the dollar and the local currency is not predicted.

Finally, let's clarify what a 6% interest rate means.
If you have a government bond that pays this much interest, you can keep it for life. Since it's a risk-free rate, there's almost no way to grow your wealth every year at this rate.

* South Korea will sell 1 trillion won a year in government bonds for personal investment from June 2024. This is because the government will create the next government bond boom after Japan.

To diversify the demand for domestic government bonds and save for retirement, the government will issue two types of bonds: 10-year and 20-year bonds. It is a strange government bond that can only be owned by individuals who can inherit it but cannot be transferred and cannot be used as collateral. Interest is paid at maturity, all at once.

If the government wants to create a government bond boom, it will need to engage celebrities with a bandwagon effect. Readers should intuitively know that you shouldn't invest in these bonds. Readers are strongly advised not to participate in this procession.

The reasons are

1) Government bonds for personal investment are absolutely safe and compound interest to maturity, and with the expectation of lower interest rates in the short term, there could be a boom in government bonds, which would cause the price of government bonds to rise more than the theoretical price.

2) The author predicts that the inflation rate will spike in the short term due to the "Powell mistake" of lowering the interest rate before the right time, followed by another sharp increase in the interest rate to calm it down.

This will cause the exchange rate to surge, causing foreigners to dump Korean government bonds and other bonds and leave the country. If we look at the period from the 1980s to

2006 in [Figure 3], we can see that there were three to four interest rate hikes and interest rates down.

If we look at the period from the 1980s to 2006 in [Figure 3], we can see that there were three to four interest rate hikes and a rate cut.

I predict that there will be at least one more round, a second government bond crash.

Needless to say, this is the best time to buy government bonds. Foreigners will be forced to dump government bonds.

Moreover, interest rates will be lowered again.

This is when the long term deflation begins in earnest.
You should realize that there is still a long period of rising prices for all bonds, including government bonds.

As for government bonds, which can only be invested by individuals for private investment, it is like giving up property rights for 10 or 20 years, so you can't even make a profit on the market.

At this point, investors who hold government bonds for private individuals are in for a real surprise, but they may be able to redeem them, subject to certain conditions. Owners of retail government bonds will find that if they hold them to maturity, the capital gains go up in smoke.

Although you won't get any market appreciation, your principal is guaranteed until maturity. While this is heartbreaking for retail investors, the government's intention is to popularize government bonds.

If the terms of issuance are not changed, the government will not be able to fulfill its purpose of currency repatriation. In the end, it will only be able to achieve its goal by abandoning the transfer and collateralization clause.

However, I believe the era of true government bond popularization will continue due to long-term deflation. By 2029 for Korea and 2048 for the rest of the world, there will be a huge bubble in government bonds. This bubble will burst when the long term deflation is resolved. When the bubble bursts, it is imperative to get out.

Also, since we are on the edge of a recession, you should always remember the viciousness of banks and other financial companies. When the economy is in a downward spiral or at the height of a recession, financial companies are at their worst.

* The evil of financial companies

Banks sold fraudulent products to unknowing small businesses and the public, and manipulated stock prices to avoid losing money. Subprime mortgage bonds were mixed and matched and sold as CODs.

Eventually, these bonds defaulted, leading to the 2008 global financial crisis. Afterward, some banks were fined heavily for this scam and even disappeared.

In South Korea, the most prominent fraud cases were the derivatives KIKO and Deutsche Bank's ELS expiry date, where they manipulated stock prices by selling them in large quantities to cause the stock price to crash. Banks, securities, insurance, etc. are for their own benefit, not for you, and you need to analyze and study financial products thoroughly to avoid being deceived.

I wonder if the reader subscribed to the Optimus Lyme Discovery scam fund during the previous government. The author has never been a member of the fund because he doesn't trust anyone, including financial companies. However, the most trustworthy financial company is the Post Office. They have so many products that we could almost call them a bank.

Even if they do sell scam products, they're the weakest of the bunch, and since the government owns 100% of the company, they can't go under. It's worth mentioning that the post office insurance is the most favorable for insurance.

* The evil of securities firms

DLS issuance is said to be in the tens of trillions of won. The amount of issuance is huge. It is dangerous because we are already in a long term deflation. This DLS is a put derivative goods. This DLS will be the main culprit of the stock market crash in the event of a major downturn.

When issuing these ELSs, brokerage firms are required to reserve about 10% of their sales to be sold short each time as a hedge. I wrote in 2018 that I believed the end of this stock market bull run would be in June 2021. And I was absolutely right.

If the composite stock index or stock prices don't fall, brokerage firms will have to pay small investors – buyers of ELS products – about four to five times the market rate for three years. That's about 8% on average. They sold an inverse margin product to the ant investors at the time of sale.

Unless they're stupid, they'll want to see their stock price or the broader stock index fall by any means necessary. Meanwhile, they've sold a product with a short-sell mandate that will induce a natural price decline.

If the price drops to the target index or target price by the expiration date, about 40% of the sales go to the brokerage firm's bottom line. If they succeed, they get a lump sum of trillions of won. If it doesn't, the brokerage firm will go under on negative margins.

Let's not forget that during Japan's 1990s crash, about four or five securities firms failed, along with many banks and insurance companies. It was during this period that the world's first "put" derivatives were sold in unlimited quantities.

Puts are the same derivative as today's DLS. It's just a different name. We're seeing the same thing with DLS and others during the major bear market that started in June 2021.

* The naive thought that financial companies, especially banks, can be trusted.

First, we use the word financial institution. Normally, an institution is a word of trust that is usually attached to a country or its neighboring institutions, such as a state agency or public institution.

However, because we are used to governed finance, we naturally use the word financial institution. In short, there is no such thing as a financial institution. It is correct to say financial companies, which are all joint-stock companies aiming for profit.

Among financial companies, banks can be trusted to manage money visibly, such as withdrawing cash or deposits and

transferring money, because I can see them immediately.
But when it comes to derivatives markets, insurance, funds, and so on, you shouldn't trust financial institutions or financial companies. Nowadays, banks sell insurance and funds. It's not their core business.

They sell these derivatives and get huge commissions from specialized financial firms, which use their extensive branch networks and access to credit to their advantage. But the public thinks these products are unique to banks.

A dollar derivative called "KIKO" was sued for fraudulent sales and went to trial, and the banks won, but I personally think it was fraudulent sales. The judge probably made a reasonable decision considering the social impact.

Financial companies' specialty products such as the Insight Fund, Brazilian government bonds, and RP dollar bonds should make investors think twice.

Contrary to their claims, you should get in the habit of thinking about what it would be like to invest upside down. They may be pushy, and they may sell foreign products without knowing the details of the product. But the responsibility lies with the investor.

Chapter 3) Why government bond bubbles happen

The reason for bubbles in bonds, especially government bonds, is that investors buy government bonds at a higher price than the theoretical price because of excessive expectations of interest rate cuts, or because they expect that interest rates will continue to fall due to long term deflation and government bonds will rise to the ceiling, as in Japan.

If the price of government bonds is higher than the theoretical price, a bubble has already formed. The price of bonds, including government bonds, automatically moves and adjusts according to interest rates. In countries where bonds don't have a lot of trading volume, this doesn't work very well.

In addition, people have different predictions of future interest rates. This creates a mismatch between the interest rate and the price of government bonds, which means that if the value and price are different, there is a bubble or a reverse bubble.

Since people's greed for more making money has no limit, the mismatch between government bonds and interest rates is often larger in times of economic fluctuations such as financial crises and foreign exchange crises. Therefore, it is natural that bubbles and reverse bubbles occur depending on economic conditions.

In normal times, that is, when the economy is moving forward with a tailwind, bubbles are almost never created.

This means that the price of government bonds does not change except for the interest component, so the investment behavior of individuals who had no interest in government bonds, except for insurance companies that need to stockpile a certain percentage of their income in bonds, corporations that need to roll over temporary surpluses, and institutional investors that need to roll over huge amounts of money, has been correct.

And,
The author's Pentagon Investing Method was published in May 2024.Until that time, government bonds and other bonds were not eligible for investment by individual investors.

With the title of " DollarSwap Fintech makes 800% profit!(5 major asset market rotation investing formula) Pentagon investment method", the investment method of government bonds has finally been summarized, and now, according to the asset cycle investment method, government bonds have become an asset that must be invested in every economic cycle, that is, once every 10 years.

In other words, in order for people to create more money than they have, in the last five steps of the Asset Cycle method, they must invest their 8x investment in government bonds one more time. From there, you can make another 1-2x return.

In a capitalist economy, when something becomes popular, bubbles spontaneously appear and disappear. The price changes around the value. If the price is lower than the value, it's an inverse bubble.

[Figure 3] is a graph of the US base rate for 70 years (1954.7.1.~2023.5.30.). It can be seen that there have been numerous bubble creation and bubble bursting periods in the government bond market since the 1980s and even before 2006.Let's look at the 1980s and pre-2006 periods separately.

This time, I will focus on the post-2006 period because we believe that the current interest rate wave started with the 2006 financial crisis.

[Figure 3] shows a schematic representation of the bubble creation and bubble bursting periods. Periods (A) and (C) are the bubble creation, and periods (B) and (D) are the bubble bursters.

(A) 〈2006-2015〉 Bubble creation time:
This is when the first bubble was created. Just before the financial crisis in 2006, the U.S. base rate was around 5%, and then the economy deteriorated so rapidly that it had to stay at 0% for about 8 years (2008-2015).

This led to a 35% surge in government bond prices on a 10-year basis. The recession forced commercial banks to stop creating credit and put the money back into excess reserves at the Fed. With nowhere else to lend the money, U.S. banks and quick investors would have bet on long-term U.S. government bonds. For more than seven years, they made really make good money.

(B) 〈2016~2019〉 The first bubble burst:
When the bubble burst, the Fed started raising interest rates in the first half of 2016, from around 0%. By July 2019, rates had risen to around 2.4%, and long-term government bonds crashed in proportion to the rate of increase. This is the first bubble burst in the post-2006 period we are looking at, i.e., the first bubble burst.

(C) 〈2019-2022〉 Bubble Creation time:
 It's bubble time again. This is part (C) of [Figure 3]. In November 2019, the coronavirus outbreak led to a 0% base rate again.

(D)〈2022~2023〉 Second bubble bursting period:
In June 2022, inflation hit 9.1% for the first time in 41 years.
The first interest rate hike of 0.25% in March 2022. The Fed was surprised and raised the rate by 0.5% in one fell swoop on May 5, 2022, and continued to raise rates until it reached 5.25% on July 27, 2023.

This is the date from March 17, 2022, the date of the first rate hike, to the start of the second bond bubble burst. This is part (D) of [Figure 3]. This time, the Fed raised the benchmark rate by a whopping 2100%, which is an incredible rate rise.

The rate hike from 0.25% in March 2022 to 5.25% on July 27, 2023. The FED has raised the interest rate by 5% in less than a year and a half. This is probably the sharpest and highest interest rate rise in history in a short period of time.

For more than 20 years, we have enjoyed low inflation due to low interest rates and China's entry into the WTO. Considering that this interest rate hike will lead to a high interest rate situation for about 40 years, the author considers this government bond bubble collapse (D) as a tipping point and categorizes it as the first collapse, even though it is the second collapse since 2016.

This collapse of the government bond bubble is seen by the author as a tipping point for future interest rates. If I consider March 17, 2022 as the tipping point for the return of high interest rates, we classify this period as the first sovereign debt bubble collapse.

Following this interest rate hike,
banks like SVB Bank and Credit Suisse Bank will start to fail. No wonder. The government bond bubble has burst. After a long period of low interest rates that created a huge bubble, the sovereign debt bubble has burst.

People are now expecting interest rates to be cut, which means that a second bubble is likely to form. So, whether it's U.S. government bonds or Korean government bonds, they're popular right now, and they're bubbling again. The July 2024 FOMC meeting hinted at the first interest rate cut in September, but not yet,I think.

Going forward, inflation will be 3-4% for at least 2-3 years and possibly 10-40 years. If interest rates continue to fall, bond prices, or government bonds, will rise sharply. But that will be two to three years from now.

For now, it's important to recognize that the excessive expectation of interest rate cuts has created another bubble in government bonds. Powell, the current Fed chairman, may decide that inflation is over and lower interest rates.

In this case, the inflation rate will spike again, and the Fed will have to raise rates again to keep up with the secondary inflation spike. This is the "Powell mistake" in the "Volcker mistake" analogy.

This is the moment when the Fed spikes rates to fight secondary inflation, and the bubble bursts again. Once any one economic entity - households, businesses, or governments - begins to collapse, the cascading effect is that the economy shrinks sharply, leading to a recession or short term deflation. With high interest rates, companies will fail one by one.

The economy then deteriorates rapidly as the long term deflation that has been underway since 2016 begins to take hold. Several countries will reach a large economic crisis of long term deflation at the same time.

At this point, foreigners are forced to sell government bonds to avoid a collapse in the price of government bonds in order to mitigate the damage of the exchange rate appreciation. We will discuss each scenario in more detail later on a case-by-case basis. This is the last time to invest in government bonds. This is when long term deflation begins in earnest.

As shown in [Figure 1], the Japanese yen was already very strong against the dollar in January 1971. Japan's long term deflation actually started with the Plaza Agreement of September 22, 1985, which the author believes ended in December 2020.

On September 22, 1985, the yen was forced to appreciate by 46% in one day, from 216.50 to 140 yen. This caused the price of Japanese imports to fall by 46%.
Japanese assets in dollar base soared by 46% overnight, although it took several years for the market to reflect....

[Figure 1] Yen to Dollar Exchange Rate Graph (1971.1.1.~2024.6.1)

The fluctuations of the yen to dollar exchange rate can be summarized in [Table 1] below.

1985. 9.	216.50 yen (Plaza Accord)
1995. 4.	84.04 yen (61% ↓)
2012. 1.	76.34 yen (64.7% ↓)
2020. 12.	107.53 yen (50.3% ↓)
2024. 5.	160.00 yen (48.8% ↑)

[Table 1] Comparison of yen and dollar exchange rates by year during the long term deflation period (1985.9 to 2024.6)

In December 2020, the yen per dollar was 107.53 yen, a 50.3% decline from the benchmark price. However, by January 2024, the dollar was around 160.00 yen due to the continued implementation of Abenomics. Compared to December 2020, when the long term deflation ended, the price of the dollar in Japan is now 48.8% higher, which means that the price of all goods and assets in Japan would have to increase by 48.8% to reflect the change in the exchange rate.

Therefore, the Japanese economy is experiencing a normalization effect. Compared to the baseline at the time of the Plaza Accord in September 1985, if your overseas investment gains are 26% or less, you are still losing money on your overseas investments, because the Plaza Accord exchange rate of 216.50-160.00 (May 2024 yen-dollar exchange rate) /216.50 X 100% = 26% is still a foreign exchange loss.

This is because you bought 1 dollar at 216.50 when you

went out to invest overseas, and when you bring the same 1 dollar back in, the local bank will only exchange it for 160.00 yen. Therefore, even if you made a profit on your investment, if your overseas investment 40 years ago did not increase by 26%, it is a loss.

This persistent drop in the dollar exchange rate always occurs in a long term deflation situation, so even if you make a small profit by investing in U.S. government bonds, you will lose a lot of money when you bring them home due to the exchange rate loss.

Japan has been unable to bring in foreign invested funds for about 40 years because of this. The author calls these dollars "ghost dollars".Since exchange losses are realized the moment you bring money into the country, they have to keep the money in local investments and use it for studying abroad or traveling to spend it without exchange losses.

Because of the exchange losses, the money could not be brought into Japan, so it became a ghost dollar floating around overseas financial markets.

With long term deflation, South Korea will experience a surge in its currency by 2029 and the rest of the world by 2048. This means that the price of the domestic dollar will continue to decline.

This is why it is recommended not to invest overseas during a long term deflation. This includes everything from foreign government bonds, foreign stocks, foreign real estate, foreign REITs, etc.

Some investors think that investing in Japan, the U.K., etc. is okay because it is not a dollar investment, but this is wrong, because all investments in the world are dollar investments, because we are all converted into dollars and then converted into local currency.

This book will cover both the formation and collapse of government bond bubbles. In a long term deflation, there is nowhere to invest. Stocks, apartments, dollars, spot prices, etc. all continue to fall as the dollar exchange rate depreciates. Very little goes up.

On the other hand, there are some financial commodities that continue to rise in price even in a long- term deflation. I am writing this book to introduce you to a financial technology (fintech) method that allows prices to rise steadily even when prices are collapsing and wealth cannot be created.

Starting in 2022, interest rates rose in a short period of time. People thought they were about to go down, so they rushed to buy government bonds in advance. So even now, after the crash, there is a bubble in government bonds. Government bonds are already down about 40-50% from their peak.

But even at today's prices, which the author believes are likely to be long term deflation, there is still at least 30-40% of the bubble left. That's because interest rates are likely to remain at current levels for at least another two to three years and possibly a decade or more.

The real interest rate on government bonds for personal investment now is negative, and there will come a time when long term deflation will be in full swing and everyone will need money.

This global deflation cannot be solved in a short period of time due to the decline in the price of the dollar, debt, and population problems, which means that short-term deflation will be followed by long-term deflation.

People's greed has always been the same in the past, present, and future. As long as people's greed for more profits remains unchanged, government bond bubbles will always be created.

Therefore, the Pentagon investment method is always valid and always correct, which means that the government bond market still has one or two more crashes and bubbles to go: two or three big crashes and two or three big bubbles.

[Figure 3] shows the interest rate evolution since 1980 and before 2006, which shows that it is impossible to fight high inflation with one single rate hike. The graph shows that there were three or four interest rate hikes after 1980 and three or four major bursts of the government bond bubble before 2006.

This book is not a book of economic theory.
It aims to guide investors on how to invest during the creation and bursting of these bubbles. Fintech (Financial Technology), or investing, is nothing more than dealing with the price fluctuations of assets as interest rates change.

I'm worried that fewer people are reading books these days due to the development of YouTubers. This means that more people are treating investing like a game.

Investors should realize that they shouldn't just look at the elephant's legs and think that it's a long beast, and invest based on short-term knowledge. You need to know the whole elephant.

Technically, we are in a long term deflation (LTD), but we are in an inflationary state due to the financial crisis and the temporary influx of money due to the coronavirus. '

Once this inflation starts to subside, the hidden deflation will kick in. Normally, deflation subsides within five years at most, but this is a long term deflation that will last longer than five years.

Just as inflation and hyperinflation are completely different, normal deflation and long term deflation have completely different investing method. In any case, I wish you all the best in becoming smart investors who know how to capitalize on crises.

In the words of Bill Gates, "It's not your fault that you were born poor, but it's your fault that you'll die poor," and that's what we're all looking for these days.

Chapter 4) Government Bond Bubbles and Modern Monetary Theory

Even if you've never been educated in economics, when we're grown up, we all know that "an increase in the quantity of money will increase prices." This is Irving Fisher's quantity theory of money.

According to mainstream economics, which supports the quantity theory of money, since 2008 and the coronavirus crisis that started in March 2020, central banks have massively supplied currency, so many times more money (M2) should have been created through credit creation.

The release of money into the real economy should have stimulated private investment, reduced unemployment, and significantly increased GDP.

Instead of flowing into the real economy, the money was returned to the Fed and accumulated as "excess reserves". This fact suggests that the conventional wisdom that "more money leads to higher inflation" was not working.

This is Modern Monetary Theory (MMT) in a nutshell. MMT was developed by Warren Mosler in the 1970s.

The theory gained attention in the wake of the 2008 global financial crisis when the U.S. central bank, the Federal Reserve, continued its $4.5 trillion in quantitative easing, creating twice as much money in just two years as the Fed had created in the previous 100 years.

MMT theorizes that it doesn't matter if the Fed creates an unlimited amount of money, as we've seen signs of deflation, not inflation, which has led to criticism that traditional monetary theory, the quantity theory of money, doesn't fit the reality. No matter how many dollars the US prints, there is no inflation.they insisted before

How would the explain the current inflation?
Well, it's because commercial banks have been unable to create credit for a while, despite the massive money printing.

In other words, they couldn't make the loans (credit creation) they liked because no one had the credit (collateral or credit) to receive the money they lent. There's no bank in the world that will lend money they can't get.

In hindsight, the MMT theory is a nonsense. The quantity theory of money is eternal. If the U.S. starts printing money, the rest of the world goes into recession.

This is Trippin's dilemma. As the U.S. current account surplus increases, the liquidity (supply) of dollars in the world decreases, causing the global economy to contract. Returning dollars to the U.S. also creates the same Triffin's dilemma.

The 2008 financial crisis released about $4.5 trillion in US dollars. As of March 2020, more than $3 trillion has been released due to the coronavirus. Even if we don't get it all back, that is, before we get it all back, the world is already in inflation and deflation at the same time. This may be the new polarization.

The Minsky moment is when accumulated debt passes a critical point, leading to a collapse in asset values and an economic crisis. With the accumulated debt of governments and households, the debt of economic entities has grown to the point where, if the trigger is pulled, the world will be in a Minsky moment overnight.

Meanwhile, recent articles suggest that the world is suffering from inflation, not deflation, and many countries are raising their economic growth forecasts.

Some argue that the world is headed for a deflationary period lasting 10-20 years or more, while others are worried about interest rate hikes due to rising inflation and economic growth. Why this divergence of views?

This is due to the base effect, whereby a relatively short-term inflationary situation is created by a temporary increase in the money supply by central banks to stimulate the economy while a long term deflation process is underway by a relatively short term inflation situation due to a temporary increase in central bank money supply to stimulate the economy.

Furthermore, the rise in economic growth and inflation rates is just a statistical reflection of the comparative slowdown during the pandemic. Don't be fooled.

Within two to three years, the global economy will rapidly plunge into deflation as the base effect fades and credit creation becomes impossible due to lack of collateral.

It is important to recognize that the amount of debt owed by countries, corporations, and individuals around the world is such that commercial banks will not be able to create credit. Without an increase in credit or collateral, no amount of money printing by central banks can increase the volume of money through credit creation.

No bank will lend money it cannot receive.
No new credit or collateral can be created unless the debts of countries, corporations, and individuals are liquidated. Banks cannot act as credit creators.

The government's debt is represented by government bonds. It borrows money from its citizens. When a government is in debt, it has issued a lot of government bonds, and it cannot digest its debt without a bubble of government bonds.

We have a chance to see how the bubble is created and how it bursts in Korea, the world's second-largest market for private government bonds after Japan.

Chapter 5) Only invest in government bonds

Bonds are not an investment asset in normal times. Of course, government bonds are also not an investment target.

Except for institutional investors with hundreds of billions of won, it was right for ordinary people to stay away from bonds until now.

In normal times, stay away from all bonds, not just government bonds!
According to the Pentagon Investing Method, you should only invest in government bonds for about 2 years every 10 years, and only in the last 5 steps, around the 8th year!

In other words, don't invest in non-government bonds forever.
There are always more investment opportunities to make more money than the small amount of interest you'd normally earn on your bonds, and bonds, including government bonds, are a very unattractive financial instrument because their prices rarely change.

However, we are now in the midst of a long term deflation.   The anticipation of a reduction in interest rates, which have risen sharply, is not the only reason why the bond market is currently in high demand.

The time when everyone needs money is coincidentally at the end of a recession, when the risk of default is very high. Whether it's households, corporations, or governments, the end of a recession is almost always the time when everyone needs money.

However, in general, all bonds, including government bonds, only become a viable investment asset in stage ⑤of the financial crisis [Figure 2]. This is because all bonds, including government bonds, rarely fluctuate in price during normal times and earn only a small amount of interest, making them unattractive to small investors of any size.

The best time to invest in government bonds is at the end of a recession, when interest rates start to fall. This means that even the safest government bonds should not be invested in normal times, but only during the fifth stage of the Pentagon Investing Method, when the recession is at its peak.

This is because a recession will soon force governments to cut interest rates, and the price of government bonds will skyrocket.

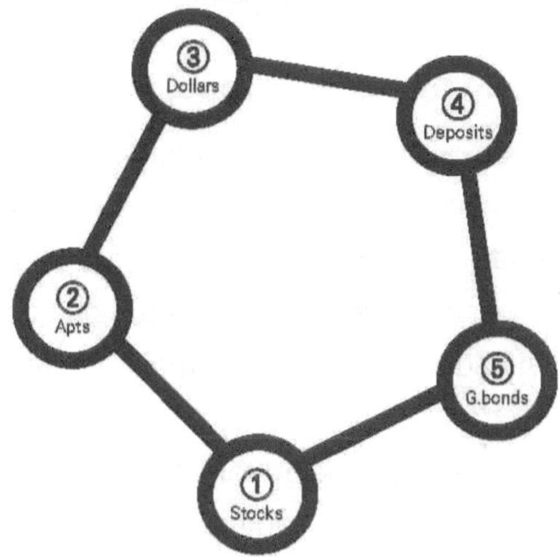

[Figure 2] Follow the Asset Cycle: Asset Cycle Investment Rotation Chart

In the end, bonds, including government bonds, should only be invested in during a severe recession. However, during a financial crisis, all fixed income investments except government bonds are extremely risky and should never be targeted.

To summarize
1) In normal times, do not invest in any bonds, including government bonds. They pay pennies on the dollar.

2) In times of crisis, all other bonds should be avoided

except government bonds, to avoid the risks of defaults, payment delays, and other risks that occur during a recession.

In particular, you should never invest in corporate bonds that suddenly increase their interest rates during a recession. When a company that normally pays a low interest rate raises the interest rate on its corporate bonds, it is already signaling that the company is risky.

3) Ultimately, with the exception of government bonds, you shouldn't invest in any bonds for life. Even government bonds should only be invested in at the end of a recession when interest rates are lower.

I don't even invest in municipal bonds. In normal times, there are many better investments available, so investing in even government bonds in a good economy is like investing in a bad economy: you lose money, i.e., there is an opportunity cost.

It is important to note that in the past, municipal bonds have often been suspended for a significant period of time due to the default of local governments in the U.S.

Therefore, bonds should only be invested in government bonds, and even then only at the end of the recession, in the Pentagon Investment method at 5 steps.

Never invest in corporate bonds, municipal bonds, etc. and always invest in government bonds, and even then, only once, at the very end of the cycle, when the government starts cutting interest rates to end the recession.

Even then, it's not too late to invest after one or two rate cuts. If you pre-emptively invest, you could lose money in July 2024, as we are now, or as Paul Volcker did. Never preemptively invest in government bonds.

A business cycle takes about 10 years to complete, so once a decade, even if it's government bonds, you should close your savings account and invest for about 2-3 years at the beginning of the cycle in government bonds, which are the last asset class in the Pentagon investment method.

Normally, government bonds are never an investment option.
According to the Pentagon Investment Method, you shouldn't invest in any asset class for the long term.

In the case of a long term deflation, the best time to sell government bonds is when you hold them for a long period of falling interest rates, enjoy the interest and capital gains, and then sell them when interest rates rise at least once or twice. Again, don't try to predict and sell ahead of time. I've never seen a government or bureaucracy so competent, nor have I ever seen a government or bureaucrat so capable of turning the economy around.

This is the beginning of a new decade of economic change, and it's time to sell government bonds and get back into stocks. Follow the asset cycle in [Figure 2]: The Asset Cycle Investment Cycle Diagram" in [Figure 2] to sell government bonds and start investing in stocks again.

4) In fact, government bonds are not always an option. Even if the 4% interest rate on a 10-year government bond goes to 0% during the fifth step of the Pentagon Investment Method, 4x7%=28% return. That's not even close to a 30% return. That's the kind of return you could make in a few hours if you invested in good stocks.

And even then, it's a once-in-a-decade opportunity. However, the Pentagon Investing Method's fifth step is to invest in government bonds because it's a time when you can't make money anywhere else.

In step 5 of the Pentagon investing method, there is nowhere to invest, like Japan in the past or South Korea today, because it is a long term deflation.

So in a short term deflation, or a recession, you should only invest in government bonds in the Pentagon Investment Method Step 5, because it's a long term deflation.

It's also a good thing to invest in government bonds because you can put your entire wealth at stake. Although the yields are low, the principal is 100% guaranteed if held to maturity, so you can invest large amounts to maximize your returns.

In conclusion, government bonds are the best investment in a long term deflation. This is because you can enjoy both interest and capital gains over a long period of time.

This pentagon investment method is a lagging investment, which means that you invest after you've seen all the results. Investments that have come full circle,it usually go up over two years or more, so you don't have to be so sensitive to one or two interest rate hikes or cuts. The key is to see the trend, invest, and avoid making a big mistake.

However, in the case of apartments, price movements are not well captured by data, so you can buy and sell with a time horizon that is six months beyond the stock index. For other assets that require rotation, such as stocks, dollars, deposits, and government bonds, price movements are visible, so you can follow the movements and invest accordingly.

However, apartments only start to rise or fall six months after the stock index rises or falls. This fact is the result of 32 years of research and analysis of the Korean economy, so the accuracy rate is almost 100%.There is no reason not to trust the prediction of apartment price changes.

Other real estate, other than apartments, will probably move more slowly than apartments due to liquidity differences. However, all assets adjust their returns similarly in the long run, so buying and selling with the trend is a safe and reliable way to invest in real estate.

Chapter 6) Another Limitation of Investing in Government Bonds

Government bonds are bonds issued by the government, so they're like cash. They pay interest every quarter, unless the government goes bankrupt.

The market price of a government bond changes with interest rates, but you get 100% of your money back at maturity. Usually, the interest rate is around 2 to 3%, and bond prices fall when rates rise and rise when rates fall.

However, while I explained in the previous chapter that you should only invest in government bonds if you expect interest rates to fall during a financial crisis or tightening, there are other limitations to investing in government bonds.

As shown in [Figure.2], during deflation, long-term government bonds are the last rotational investment goods in the asset market, according to the Pentagon Investing Method.

It is the asset with the highest guaranteed return, so you should never forget the figures of the change in the price of government bonds as interest rates change.⑤ At this stage, all assets except government bonds are falling in price.

This is the time to take the opportunity to invest in government bonds and make a killing. This information on market price differentials due to interest rate changes was only shared by bond rating companies and institutional investors. In Korea, there are three or four bond rating companies that specialize in credit ratings.

In a short term deflation or a long term deflation, the last step of the Pentagon investing method, Step ⑤, is to invest only in government bonds. Any other asset will lose money.

Summarizing these facts, we have the Big 5 investment asset rotation cycle of stocks -> apartments -> dollars -> savings -> government bonds that has been created by human greed for hundreds of years, and if you break it, you will lose big.
We've discussed the limitations of investing in government bonds in the previous chapter, but there are other limitations as well.

1) The bond price is different from the theoretical price.
As the interest rate changes, the bond price should change exactly according to the formula. It is common in countries with small bond issuance and weak bond liquidity that prices do not form according to this formula. In other words, except for the United States and the United Kingdom, government bond market prices are always distorted.

Outside of the U.S., government bonds are usually in low supply, and a small number of institutional investors hold the majority of bonds, which prevents fair pricing in response to interest rate changes. In order to develop the bond market in countries other than the United States, it is necessary to have a liquidity provider.

There are two separate markets for stocks and bonds. It can be traded through the HTS system of securities companies. In this case, trading government bond ETFs on the stock market has a similar effect to buying and selling actual government bonds.

There are some government bond ETFs listed on the stock market. Therefore, in Korea, where the bond market is underdeveloped due to the low volume of bonds in circulation and the lack of a fair price, you can buy and sell bond ETFs.

Buying and selling through them can have a similar effect to owning the actual government bonds. There are short-term bond ETFs, such as the government bond, 3-year ETF government bond, 5-year ETF government bond, 10-year ETF government bond, 20-year ETF government bond, and so on.

However, these bond ETF products have a limitation that bond investors cannot take a strategy of holding the bonds to maturity, as the securities company always replaces the bonds with government bonds of the same yield or government bond futures to match the maturity of the ETF product, such as 2-10 years. Also, it is not always clear if the full amount of interest is paid out each time.

As Long Term Deflation progresses, interest rates will continue to fall steadily. In response, government bond prices will skyrocket and skyrocket. The author believes that Korea's long term deflation will end in 2029 and the rest of the world's long term deflation will end around 2048.

During long term deflation, the relative value of cash continues to rise.This doesn't mean that the value of cash is actually increasing.

It means that the relative price of cash is rising because the price of everything else in the world is falling - real estate, stocks, commodities, gold, silver, etc. This increases the purchasing power of cash. That's why cash is the best.

Even if cash earns almost no interest, there's no question which is better because government bonds increase in price every year in addition to the interest they promise.

In Japan, where long term deflation lasted 32 years, interest rates were consistently lowered to negative rates. The world, including South Korea, has been experiencing long term deflation since January 2016.

I expect South Korea's interest rates to fall to negative rates in the near future, just like Japan's. During a long term deflation, investors continue to hold government bonds and earn interest income. In addition, capital gains from falling interest rates will increase.

In the case of short term deflation, If the annual balance of payments was in surplus a year ago,investors should immediately start investing in stocks. In a procyclical manner, that is, governments start raising interest rates once the deflation is over and the economy is improving.

When the government raises the benchmark interest rate, it's like telling us that deflation (recession) is over. This means that when the government raises interest rates, the price of government bonds will go down, so it's clear that you should sell your bonds and start investing in stocks again, following the first step of the Pentagon Investing Method. Another decade of investing begins.

But don't be in a hurry. It's not too late to start investing after you've seen one or two interest rate hikes. It's better to invest in stocks after you've seen a positive balance of payments a year ago and the three line break.

In particular, in the case of long term deflation, it is better to take a step back than to enter the stock market immediately when the balance of payments shows a one-year annual trade surplus. I think it is safer to sell long term government bonds and start investing in stocks after one or two government rate hikes.

Long term deflation always starts with short term deflation. A clear exit from long term deflation should be judged by the restoration of the proportional relationship between the dollar index price and the international gold price.

The best time to invest in government bonds is when a recession is in full swing. This is because they are an investment that only increases in price when interest rates go down.

Of course, interest is paid even in normal times, but if there is no market differential, government bonds are not very attractive aside from stability.

2) In addition, Korea will introduce a financial investment income tax next year. Capital gains will also be taxed differently than in the past, so this is a new limitation of investing in government bonds.

You should consider the pros and cons of investing in government bonds and decide whether to invest or not.

Chapter 7) The government bond market freaking out over a quarter-point change in interest rates. Why?

Here's why a mere 0.25% change in interest rates can send the bond market into a tailspin! Here's why a mere 0.25% change in interest rates can send the bond market into a tailspin!

For a 10-year government bond, the price of the bond will rise and fall by about 7% as interest rates rise and fall by 1%, as shown in [Table 2] below.

The reason why we use the words "surge" and "crash" for this 7% price change is that when investing in government bonds, you usually invest a large amount of money because it is safe enough to bet your entire fortune, so the total amount of loss or profit is huge.

Also, since government bonds are an asset that rarely fluctuate in price during normal times, a 0.25% change in interest rates can cause the price to jump as much as 1.75% on the 10-year government bond.

Let's say someone owns 10,000 won worth of government bonds with a current interest rate of 2%, and the government suddenly issues another bond with a 3% interest rate.

It is obvious that everyone will want to buy the 3% bond because it pays 1% more interest than the 2% bond. That's a 1% difference in interest. Well, no one will buy an existing 2% government bond unless you reduce the price by the equivalent of 1%, over the life of the bond.

This is because the same money can be used to buy a new government bond with a 3% interest rate bond. Therefore, when interest rates rise, the price of already issued government bonds will have to fall to adjust to the increased interest rate. For the same reason, a decrease in interest rates will cause the price of government bonds to increase.

The key information is that the price of a 20-year bond will increase by 14% and a 30-year bond will increase by 21% when interest rates fall by 1%. In the opposite case, when interest rates rise, bond prices fall proportionally.

Since the market trades at the present value (NPV) of the total amount of interest to be received in the future, the actual price is slightly lower than the calculated price, i.e., 10,000 won in 10 years is not worth the same as 10,000won today.

Therefore, it is natural that the actual price in the market is slightly different from the calculated price simply because the market discounts future prices.

Since the future price is discounted and traded in the present, it is natural that the actual price in the market will be slightly different from the price calculated by simply (interest rate difference × residual term).

If you take the 10 year bond as a reference, if the interest rate goes up or down by 1%, that is, (3%-2%)=1%, you would think that there should be a 10% difference in price because it is a 10 year bond, but 1% in 10 years is not the same as 1% now.

Therefore, the market calculates the future interest equivalent as the Net Present Value, which is about 7% (Depends on the discount rate, but for a 10 year bond, it's actually around 7.8%.), so there is not much difference.

As of October 2023, U.S. government bond prices for maturities longer than 10 years have dropped 46% from their peak in March 2020 and 53% for 30-year government bonds in just three and a half years, according to Bloomberg. This is because interest rates have risen from 0.25% to 5.25%.

We don't know how much further government bond prices will fall. The author predicts that in the long run, they will fall by at least 30-40% more. Of course, there is no doubt that this will be followed by a long period of bubbles. During this period, there will be another huge bubble.

[Table 2] shows the percentage change in bond prices up and down for a 1% increase or decrease in interest rates. Interest rates and government bond prices are inversely correlated.

5 yrs	3.5%
10 yrs	7%
20 yrs	14%
30 yrs	21%

[Table 2] Percentage change in the price of bonds and other government bonds in response to a 1% increase/decrease in the benchmark interest rate

All government bonds have a pre-determined interest rate when they are issued. Therefore, government bonds may not be a safe haven asset. This is explained in more detail in [Chapter 8].

The interest rate on a government bond will be similar to the actual market rate at the time. If the market rate is 5%, government bonds are safe, so you should issue them at a rate just under 5%, i.e., 4.5% would be about right. If you issue it at 4%, it will be indigestible, and if you issue it at 5%, people will try to buy each other.

In Korea, both the issuance market and the secondary market for government bonds are still underdeveloped, making it difficult to buy or sell government bonds easily.

Currently, it is possible to directly buy and sell national housing bonds, government bonds, regional development bonds such as Seoul Metro bonds, Gangwon-do regional development bonds, KEPCO bonds, various bank bonds, bonds of securities companies, and corporate bonds of individual companies, but there is not enough selling volume to directly buy and sell, and there are not many buying forces, so the buying and selling price is not well formed, so it is inconvenient to buy and sell.

However, if you live off of interest payments every quarter or six months, you're better off buying directly, and indirect investments like government bonds through ETFs are not my personal favorite.

However, there are now bond-related ETFs that pay interest on a monthly basis. If you want to capitalize on interest rate movements and receive interest directly, the only way to do so is through direct trading on an HTS.

If you expect interest rates to fluctuate, buying and selling government bonds in anticipation of interest rate movements can be an attractive investment, as it allows you to lock in both the annual coupon rate and the price difference when you sell.

The world has been in a period of falling interest rates for about 40 years. Some countries have even had negative interest rates in the past, including Denmark, and Japan was one of the last to adopt them./

The world has been in a period of falling interest rates for about 40 years. As shown in [Figure 3], this has been the case since the 1980s, with Denmark and Japan being the latest countries to adopt negative interest rates.

Zero or negative interest rates are the predominant interest rate between commercial banks and the central bank. Commercial banks are required to deposit cash in excess of a certain amount of marketable funds with the central bank as a reserve for payments. The central bank then pays a negative interest rate on the money they deposit.

It's a way to encourage the public to lend money to revitalize a sluggish economy. There is an argument that we will be in an era of high interest rates for the next 40 years, so I think we should make a different prediction and invest accordingly.

The inflation rate in the US was 9.1%, so the base rate was raised continuously to keep the inflation rate within 2%, reaching from 0.25% to 5.25% in a short period of time. Usually, the real tax rate on government bonds has been trending downward for three to four months before the base rate peaks, but I think this time is different,

This is because the author respects the minority view of Ray Dalio and others that the 2% inflation target is unlikely to be achieved, contrary to the expectations of the Federal Reserve. The average inflation rate is more likely to be stuck around 3-4%.

As a result, we believe that the benchmark interest rate is likely to rise to an average of 8-9% or higher.

In other words, it will be a big mistake to invest in government bonds beforehand, as the era of high interest rates will last for a long time, which is completely different from hopes and predictions.

Therefore, I recommend that you wait for one or two real cuts in interest rates after the "Volcker's mistake" before investing in government bonds.

This is why forecasting interest rates is essential when investing in fixed income, including government and corporate bonds. The time to invest in bonds according to the Pentagon Investment Method, which follows the flow of money between the five major assets (stocks, apartments, dollars, savings, and government bonds), always coincides with the entry of the last of the five assets into a full-blown recession.

Therefore, since we are investing in bonds during a recession, we consider all bonds other than government bonds, such as municipal, bank, and corporate bonds, to be risky. This is why you should only invest in government bonds.

The question arises whether U.S. government bonds are the safest asset class, as the SVB crisis was triggered by the collapse of the 10-year U.S. government bond due to interest rate fluctuations. Of course, this has little to do with the safety of US government bonds themselves.

However, long-term government bonds are a risky asset because their price fluctuates too much when interest rates change. There is no price safety.

For government bonds to be an absolute safe haven, they need to have a maturity of one to two years before they are equivalent to cash or cash equivalents.

However, if the maturity is less than a year or two away, it is too short to generate any capital gains. Even when investing in government bonds, you need to build a portfolio between short- and long-term government bonds.

Going forward, there is always the possibility that Japan will raise interest rates, or that the euro will depreciate, causing U.S. government bond yields to rise sharply as it sells U.S. government bonds to defend its exchange rate.

This is because neither South Korea, Japan, nor China will be able to maintain the value of their currencies by selling U.S. government bonds or reserves to maintain the value of their currencies.

Add to that the fact that U.S. government bonds are held by every regional bank and central bank in the U.S. and by large banks around the world as safe investments or as foreign exchange reserves.

Almost all of the world's blue-chip banks have been implicated in the collapse of US government bond prices in the wake of the US rate hike, so naturally, a 0.25% change in interest rates will result in hundreds of billions of dollars in losses and gains.

Venture capitalists and tech companies always have a lot of debt.

Therefore, interest rates and venture companies are mutually exclusive. When interest rates rise, it is normal for the Nasdaq index, which contains tech stocks, to fall. It's a simple fact that you should always keep in mind when investing in stocks.

Chapter 8) How High Can Government Bonds Go?

In the future, if the profit from the sale of stocks exceeds 50 million won, it will be taxed from the following year. Starting next year, gains on the sale of bonds will be taxed if they exceed 2.5 million won, but dividend and interest income will not be taxed.

If interest rates fall by 1% on the 10-year benchmark, the price of government bonds rises by 7%. The 20-year government bond would jump 14% on the spot.

A 30-year government bond would jump about 21%. Of course, as interest rates rise, the price of government bonds drops at each of these rates. It is always important to remember that the duration calculation is based on the remaining term.

So far this year, short-term investments of a few hundred million can be very profitable if you correctly predict interest rate movements. If you invest in a 2-3% interest rate differential during a period of falling interest rates, you can enjoy a large time value of money and annual interest.

Plus, government bonds are absolutely safe, so you can

bet your life savings on them. Investing in government bonds is also a great way to invest in large trading amounts and not take into account capital gains, meaning that you don't have to buy or sell, and you can live a comfortable retirement with interest until maturity.

However, if inflation persists and interest rates continue to rise before maturity, their value will drop dramatically. This is what happened to Silicon Valley Bank (SVB) in the US in 2023 or the bankruptcy of Signature Bank.

Unrealized capital gains will slowly disappear until maturity, so the price will crash over time. At maturity, you always get back only the face value.

The world, including South Korea, has been in a deflationary economy since January 2016, with the exception of Japan. In this case, government bonds are the best investment.

Cash is also a good investment, but bank deposits pay low interest, which is not the case with government bonds, and government bonds also come with a huge capital gains premium.

Even if you buy a bond at the wrong time and it turns out to be a loss at market valuation, if you hold it to maturity, you will be paid back the face value with interest. Cash increases in relative value, but you can't profit from capital gains. This makes government bonds a more attractive investment than cash.

In Japan, the interest rate on 10-year government bonds was around 2.5% in 1995, but as of May 2023, it was negative at -0.1%. As of July 2024, +0.1% is the benchmark interest rate in Japan.

Compared to 1995, the price of Japan's 10-year government bonds would have theoretically increased by more than 17%. This can be seen in [Figure 4], which shows the evolution of the interest rate of the Japanese 10-year government bond.

The 17% increase is simply a capital gain due to yield differentials, not to mention the 2.5% annualized interest income. Other prices continued to fall.

The 17% increase is simply market gains due to yield differentials, not to mention the 2.5% interest earned each year. Not to mention that other prices have been falling steadily.

Korea also has two or three 30-year government bonds, and you can trade listed government bonds directly using the securities company's home trading system. A 50-year government bond has also been issued. The only problem is that there isn't a lot of buyers and sellers. This means that a fair price cannot be established.

Government bond price prediction case study

Calculate the price of a 30-year Korean government bond with a surface rate of 2% as interest rates change. If the market interest rate on government bonds becomes negative, i.e. -0.1%, as in Japan, this bond will increase by more than 42% (about 2×21%). The 42% increase means that the bond will be traded at a premium, i.e., the market price of a 10,000 won bond will be around 14,200 won.

Imagine an inverse interest rate rise, i.e., an issue yield of 2% and a secondary yield of 4%. The 30-year government bond would be priced around 5,800 won. (4%-2%)X21%=42% because it drops by 42%. Compare the yield to a time deposit.

If the government bond issue rate today is 0.02%, the interest rate on a commercial CD would be around 0.02% per year (yield). If the interest rate on already issued government bonds is 2% per year, what should be the trading price of these bonds?

To earn 200 won per year on a government bond with

a term deposit, you need a term deposit of 1 million won.

1,000,000×0.02%=200 won, which is the real interest rate in the market. So, in this case, what should be the actual trading price per 10,000,000 won of an already issued government bond with an interest rate of 2%?

1,000,000 won?
14,200 won?

If you account for the bond at KRW 1 million, you will have to write down the value by about KRW 100,000 per year for the remaining life of the bond. This is because no matter what the market price is, the government will only receive 1,000 won per bond and 200 won in interest at maturity.

Now consider the implications of a 6% interest rate.
Let's say a 10-year government bond is issued at 10,000 won per bond and a normal interest rate of 2%. Depending on the interest rate situation, the price of this bond could fluctuate between 3,000 and 12,000 won.

Further downward and upward movements are also possible. A 10,000 won government bond would have to trade at 3,300 won to yield 6%. The return is calculated relative to the investment amount.That is, interest (200 won)/investment(3,300 won)×100%=6.00 return.

With a 100% safe and risk-free rate of return, you can bet your entire life savings. Simple compounding calculations show that it only takes 12 years to double your investment.

Let's also calculate what happens if interest rates fall.
If interest rates fall by 1%, this bond trades at 1,700 won, and if they fall by 2%, it trades at 1,400 won. If the rate goes to negative 1% due to deflation like in Japan... it becomes 12,100 won.

But in reality, the transaction price is what you call value. Because in deflation, the purchasing power of cash skyrockets every year, because government bonds are like cash with interest, and no one will sell them until they mature, which means they become priceless, just like Japanese government bonds.

In the end, despite the low interest rates, it's important to understand when you should buy and when you should sell government bonds: when interest rates go down, buy them, and when interest rates go up, sell them.

However, it is recommended to follow the Three Times Principle, i.e., when interest rates rise two or three times, rather than making a decision based on a single change in interest rates. These are the main points of investing in government bonds.

Government bonds are a risk-free, profitable asset that performs this magic as interest rates fluctuate. They are also used as a basis for avoiding taxes because they are effectively bearer bonds and can be cashed out and given to children.

There are few better investments than long-term government bonds, where the interest rate fluctuations can secure interest rates above the monthly rent of an income-producing property.

Moreover, Korea's government bonds are about to enter a long period of deflation, and there is a very good chance that they will continue to rise until at least 2029.

In the end, we can see that all assets, including stocks and apartments, which are typical investment assets, are adjusted by the "Invisible Hand" of Adam Smith as interest rates change.

Different types of assets adjust at different times, but in the end, they all adjust to the rate of return.

The basis of the yield calculation is the interest rate. Exchange rates also have a big impact on the price of goods, such as economic fluctuations, but they are closely related to interest rates.

Chapter 9) **Trading government bonds in the real market**

Japanese government bonds are currently the most expensive bonds in the world. The Japanese central bank is buying unlimited amounts of 10-year government bonds at a yield of 2%. But no one is selling.

A government bond with a face value of 10,000 won due to a fall in interest rates could theoretically be worth 1 million won, as in the example in [Chapter 8], but whether it actually trades at this price or whether there are financial firms or individuals willing to buy it is another matter.

It's not hard to imagine that Japan's government and corporate bond markets have long since become dead markets with no trading. Japanese government bonds are currently on the edge of pricelessness. At some point, South Korea will be like Japan.
This is because government bonds will not be tradable on the market.

Even this data for Japan is not widely known, and the

author found it himself, and it is relatively accurate with some errors. Korean economists, theorists, and credit rating agency practitioners keep these crucial numbers to themselves.

Even if you want to buy government bonds, Korea doesn't have a well-established government bond market, and bond quotes from securities companies are a bit suspicious. In this case, the best way to invest in government bonds is through government bond ETFs.

However, bond-related ETFs do not invest in actual bonds, but in bond yields ratios or bond futures. You are always investing in the yields or futures of a group of bonds with the same remaining maturity, i.e. a 10-year bond ETF is a 10-year bond ETF forever.

With the exception of government bonds, which are for personal investment only, you can invest in bonds that pay interest periodically. Recently, there are bond ETFs that pay interest on a monthly basis.

These include KODEX 10-Year Government Bond, KODEX 10-Year Government Bond Inverse, KOSEF 10-Year Government Bond, and KOSEF 10-Year Leveraged.

Since bonds are favorable, retail investors seem to be

investing in U.S. long-term bond ETFs. However, technically, U.S. long-term bond ETFs do not directly invest in U.S. bonds. Rather, they invest in U.S. bond yields or bond index futures.

If you look closely, there's actually a big difference between the two.

(a) If you bought a 10-year U.S. government bond directly, you would receive interest at the annualized surface rate, and at maturity, you would receive the principal amount of the bond.

(b) If you bought a 10-year U.S. government bond ETF, the annual ETF dividend is about 2%. The ETF has no maturity and expires on the day you sell it. It's a product that aims to achieve market price gains rather than dividends, and its price movements depend on the direction of bond yields.

Most importantly,
1) To make a big profit from investing in government bonds, i.e., to make a jackpot, you need to buy long-term government bonds while rates are falling and then sell them when rates stop falling.

For a 30-year government bond, whether spot or ETF, 3 x 7% = 21% per 1% decrease in interest rates, but there are almost no 30-year government bonds, so there is no 30-year ETF.

2) In this case, if you buy and sell spot, it is highly unlikely that you will be able to move with the theoretical price because it is not liquid enough, i.e. the volume of 30-year government bonds is too low to create a proper price. This is because a significant amount of 30-year government bonds are owned by only a few brokerage firms, which may be impossible to buy or sell.

You can buy and sell bonds on a brokerage firm's HTS in real time, but the price is almost always different from the theoretical price.

However, if you can buy and sell at a fair price, it's best to own physical government bonds. This is because you get to enjoy both the fixed interest and the market gains.

3) Even if the price of government bonds is expected to increase significantly due to the long-term drop in interest rates, it is advantageous to buy and sell ETFs rather than not being able to enjoy the market price difference due to the lack of long-term government bonds in the market.

ETFs may be slightly different in price, but they are still a product that allows you to take full advantage of the market price difference, as the price reflects the fluctuations in bond yields and bond futures prices.

You should also distinguish between physical ETFs and futures ETFs for government bonds, as there are not many of them in the market, making it inconvenient to buy and sell.

4) Since U.S. government bond ETFs invest in U.S. dollars, it is not recommended to invest in U.S. government bond ETFs because the price of the dollar will collapse in the long term like in Japan during long term deflation.

In addition, there are various taxes, so investing in US government bond ETFs is risky. In the end, your investment will be a ghost dollar.

For example, Korea,
Since it is difficult to buy government bonds that match the market price, it is judged that it is necessary to buy a long-term government bond ETF product and take advantage of the market price difference when the secondary crash of government bonds is in full swing, i.e., when bond yields skyrocket.

In addition, I wonder if intermediate sales and mortgages of government bonds will be allowed, as the volume of government bonds for individual ownership cannot be fully consumed. In this case, I expect to be able to buy government bonds for individual ownership at the market price.

It is important to note that with the introduction of the Financial Investment Income Tax, capital gains from the sale of government bonds will be subject to the Financial Investment Income Tax, which is the same as capital gains tax,

And nowadays, government bonds are not issued in physical form. They have long since become e-bonds, which means they only exist online, but they are guaranteed by the government and are therefore absolutely safe.

Chapter 10) Government bond market gains disappear like smoke at maturity

1) My readers should be aware that, according to the asset market's cyclical investment sequence, if you buy government bonds in step ⑤ and realize a price gain due to a drop in interest rates, you will lose the price gain if you hold them until maturity.

Therefore, you should sell when the interest rate is at its lowest point, i.e. when the price of government bonds is at its highest point.

2) On the other hand, if you buy government bonds that have already fallen due to rising interest rates and hold them until maturity, you can enjoy all the gains. In this case, you will enjoy the profit until maturity at a higher interest rate than your investment, and you will be refunded the par value at maturity.

So, in this case, you're taking advantage of the capital gain, which means that the best time to buy government bonds, which are the only fixed-income investment, is when the price of government bonds has fallen, i.e. when the price of government bonds has fallen enough.

In addition, if a country experiences a financial crisis, currency crisis, or a general decline in popularity, foreigners will have to dump their government bonds to avoid currency exchange losses and falling prices. For domestic residents, this is the best opportunity to invest in government bonds at the cheapest price and for the long term.

A specific example is Paul Volcker in the 1980s.

In December 1980, at the end of the third inflation wave, the peak yield (interest rate) on U.S. government bonds was a whopping 22%. If you had invested in US government bonds in 1981, you could have earned 22% for 30 years. That's unthinkable today.

In 1974, i.e. during the Paul Volcker era, the inflation rate was (11.0%), and in 2022, the inflation rate is (9.1%). What will be the peak government bond yield of the third wave? Predict.

Using a simple proportional equation, the expected peak rate in this inflationary escape is a whopping 18.7%. That's a panic-level recession. The author is predicting the beginning of a long term deflation.

Chapter 11) The first wave of the government bond bubble has already passed.

In the US, the base interest rate jumped by 2,100% (21x) from 0-0.25% to 5.25%. US government bonds should have crashed 35% on a 10-year basis. Long term government bonds are therefore risky assets, not safe-haven assets.

We have learned from the US government's actions after the SVB bank failure that long-term government bonds are not safe. In other words, they are no longer a safe haven. They are only safe if you hold them to maturity. This is due to the price crash when interest rates rise.

However, the first phase of the US government bond bubble has already passed, as the first rate hike has already passed. Of course, the government bond bubble burst that the author is referring to also occurred in the 1980s.

However, to avoid confusion, we have already mentioned that I decided to call the collapse of the government bond bubble on May 5, 2022, the date of the first interest rate hike, the first collapse.

This is because I believe that May 5, 2022 was the tipping point of the era of high interest rates (not the era of negative or 0% interest rates), meaning that the first crash has already passed.

However, I believe we are still in the midst of the second and third government bond bubble bursts, just like in the 1980s.

Since the SVB default in the US in 2023, US Treasury Secretary Janet Yellen has long been in favor of recognizing US government bonds at face value, regardless of their current value. This temporary measure is now over.

Without it, many local banks in the US would have failed. US government bonds should now be valued at market. If US government bonds were marked-to-market, many local banks would be insolvent. This measure ended in May 2024. It will now be marked-to-market.

The largest holders of U.S. government bonds are, by far, regional banks. Governments also hold a significant percentage of their foreign reserves in U.S. government bonds.

It is also important to note that the price drop in US government bonds is not reflected in their foreign reserves.

As part of UBS's recent M&A transaction of Swiss Credit Suisse, perpetual corporate bonds issued by Swiss Credit Suisse were extinguished for free. The perpetual bonds issued by the supposedly safe bank were wiped out for nothing.

Perpetual bonds are also known as new capital securities. This is a monster corporate bond, just like government bonds for personal investment. It can be burned, demoted, increased, etc. in favor of the issuer without any compensation.

Currently, Korean steelmaker POSCO, KEPCO, former Doosan Heavy Industries and Construction, and some Korean banks have issued perpetual bonds.

 It is important to check the issuance terms, conversion terms, and burning terms before buying or selling. No investor will read all the terms and conditions.

I think a big loss awaits here as well. The recent sale of HMM did not go through because of the new capital bonds already issued. The whole world is a minefield if you look closely. Therefore, you should never make investments based on popular YouTube videos and fragmented economic knowledge.

Now it's time to dive into the final step, investing in government bonds, which is the fifth and final step in the Pentagon method of investing, which tracks the flow of money between the five main assets: stocks, apartments, dollars, savings, and government bonds.

In the meantime, the money you've earned over the past eight years under the Pentagon Investing Method should already be in a savings account at a bank or, if you're impatient, in government bonds.

If not, it's time to close your time deposits and start investing in government bonds now that the government has lowered the benchmark interest rate.

There's no telling how far this rate cut will go, as the country has already been in the midst of a long term deflation since January 2016.

US government bonds are generally considered a risk-free asset, which is why governments hold some of their foreign exchange reserves in US government bonds.

However, as the SVB (Silicon Valley Bank) bankruptcy shows, there is no such thing as a safe asset, and US government bonds can be both safe and very risky.

While Japan's asset market collapsed in tandem with the decline of its core working-age population starting in 1990, Japan's working-age population actually began to decline in earnest in 1995.

In South Korea, the core working-age population began to decline in 2013, and the working-age population began to decline in 2016. The U.S. and Europe began shrinking their working-age populations in 2006, a decade earlier than we did.

Given the long term deflation trend, I believe that Korea will enter negative interest rates like Japan. This is a really scary situation. We can't even return to normal interest rates in the short term.

Long term deflation is so destructive because it is caused by a decline in the working-age population, especially the full retirement of baby boomers, massive household debt, and a triple set of outdated mortgage rules with request for reimbursement

It took Japan's Tankai generation (6.8 million people born between 1947 and 1949) only 32 years to escape the long term deflation caused by recession and household debt etc!

Moreover, Korea's long term deflation will be stronger and faster than Japan's long term deflation. The reason for this is in people's structure. You can see this by looking at the number of baby boomers in Korea and their percentage of the total population.

Japan's Tankai generation has 400,000 fewer people than South Korea's baby boomers (born between 1955 and 1963, 7.2 million). As a percentage of the total population, Japan is also one-third smaller than South Korea's 14.4% baby boomer population, at 5.7%.

If you do the math, and if population is the biggest reason for deflation, as Harry Dent claims, then it is obvious that deflation will progress 2.5 times faster in South Korea than in Japan (14.4%/5.7%=2.5 times).

Therefore, the side effects of long term deflation due to population issues will be stronger in South Korea compared to Japan, meaning that the side effects of Japan's lost 32 years will be reached in only 12 years (32/2.5=12.8 years).

This is because Japan has a population of 120 million, about 2.5 times larger than Korea's 50 million. Even a long term deflation phenomenon would come quickly in South Korea.

However, there's another factor to consider.

While Japan's Tankai generation is concentrated in three years, Korea's baby boomers are spread out over nine years, which means that the progression of long term deflation could be faster or not as expected.

No one knows exactly how long Korea's long term deflation will last, but in the author's opinion, it will last until 2029 (32 years/2.5 years=12.8 years).

If Korea loses 32 years like Japan, it would take until 2016+32 years=2048 to become the Japan we are today. However, if we consider the proportion of the Tankai and Baby Boomer generations to the total population of each country, 32 years in Japan is about 32 years/2.5 years=12.8 years in Korea.

In the author's judgment, it will last until 2029 (32 years/2.5 years=12.8 years).If the demographics are no different from Japan's, Korea's long term deflation will also last 32 years, so it may end in 2048.

However, given the proportion of the Tankai and Baby Boomer generations to the total population, it is reasonable to assume that 32 years in Japan would be about 32 years/2.5 years=12.8 years in Korea.

Since the Baby Boomers are evenly distributed over 9 years and the Tankai Generation is concentrated in 3 years, 2016 plus 12.8 years will be around 2029, which is the author's arbitrary estimate that Korea will be completely out of long term deflation around 2029.

Of course, the author could be wrong. One of the reasons is that South Korea's second wave of baby boomers (born between 1964 and 1974, 9.5 million people) have also started to retire.

When this population retires, it is predicted to reduce South Korea's economic growth by 0.38%. On the other hand, the reunification of South and North Korea could add 21 million people to the population at once, so there are quite a few variables.

But while Japan has lost 32 years, the rest of the world has 32 years to lose. We also need to take into account that the total debt-to-GDP ratio needs to return to roughly 100% for the economy to be revitalized.

Despite the complexity of the estimates, it's easy to recognize when a long term deflation period has begun and when it has ended by using indicators.

A country's exit or entry into a long-run deflation is indicated when the proportional relationship between the domestic US dollar price and the KOSPI index returns to an inverse relationship, indicating that the long term deflation has ended, and vice versa.

Since 2016, we can see that the exchange rate and the price of gold and crude oil have been proportional. If it becomes inversely proportional, then we are back to an inflationary economy (normal economy, short term deflation).

Now let's talk about US government bonds!
In March 2023, the 40-year-old Silicon Valley Bank (SVB), the 16th largest bank in the United States, collapsed in just 36 hours with a bank run no touch run. Around the same time, Signature Bank of the United States also failed.

First Republic Bank was also hit by touchrun (where bankrun means going to a bank to withdraw funds, touchrun means withdrawing funds without going to a bank, just by tapping an app on their smartphone). SVB is the second largest bank in the U.S. in terms of the number of banks that have closed on the brink of failure.

What's even more surprising is that SVB's crisis was caused by its heavy investment in 10-year U.S. government bonds, a supposedly safe and risk-free asset. In just over a year, the US base rate increased by 2,100% (21 x) from 0-0.25% to 5.00-5.25% in March 2023. The sustained rate hike resulted in $1.8 billion in unrealized valuation losses on SVB's heavily held 10-year US government bonds.

If a bank or country had $10 billion or so invested in U.S. 10-year government bonds, how much would it have lost?

(5.25-0.25) × 7%=35%, or a $3.5 billion valuation loss. Because of the way government bonds are valued, if interest rates fall by 1%, the price of the 10-year government bond instantly drops by 7%. A 20-year government bond would immediately drop 14% per 1%. A 30-year bond would drop 21% per 1%. The calculation is the same for the reverse case.

Government bonds, supposedly a risk-free asset, are not so safe. Moreover, even the world's safest asset, U.S. government bonds, have seen their value collapse due to a spike in unrealized losses, causing banks to fail.

People say that the Big Four banks are safe, but in fact, they have the largest holdings of U.S. government bonds. In the end, there seems to be no way for anyone to avoid risk.

The US will try to protect US government bonds at all costs, even if it means giving up inflation protection. Already, the U.S. government has launched the Bank Term Funding Program (BTFP), which allows the government to buy 10-year U.S. government bonds at par, regardless of market price, and lend them to small and medium-sized local banks for one year at a rate in the mid-4% range, within a $2 trillion limit.

There was $4.5 trillion released during the subprime and about $2.5 trillion released during the coronavirus. You have to realize that $2 trillion in BTFP is a lot of money when you're dealing with 9.1% inflation.

It's also the opposite of what they're doing now, which is tightening monetary policy. It's a sign that inflation can be expected to continue for a longer period of time, and it's a strong statement of intent to protect U.S. government bonds through a longer period of high interest rates.

In other words, it would be a laughable situation to go back to QE during QT (Quantitative Tightening). In the end, it would be like the U.S. abandoning its inflationary defense, and inflation would spike back up to 15% or so, according to bond king Gundlach.

There are arguments that QE is not related to inflation because it is only within the banking system, but it will eventually be released to the real economy. If the inversion of short- and long-term interest rates is reversed again due to a recession, the economy will rapidly decline within 4 to 6 months.

When there is a divergence between long- and short-term interest rates, it becomes a recession because banks usually sell time deposits and bank bonds to raise short-term funds and lend money for a long period of time, securing profits from the difference in interest rates.

In other words, banks lend short-term funds to raise long-term funds and earn profits from the difference in interest rates.

When short-term and long-term interest rates are inverted, banks are unable to create credit because they cannot raise short-term funds, which in turn prevents them from lending long-term funds, which leads to a recession.

Without the ability to create credit, banks lose a lot of revenue. If this period is extended, not only will banks face a crisis, but the economy will suffer.

Currently, Japan's YCC (short for Yield Curve Control, a monetary policy that predetermines the interest rate on government bonds of a certain maturity and buys or sells government bonds to keep it at that level) policy provides unlimited purchases of 10-year government bonds, and as of April 2023, the purchase rate was 109% of the government bonds outstanding.

More purchases than issuance means that 9% of the 10-year government bonds were shorted, meaning that hedge funds were shorting Japanese government bonds.

This is shorting in anticipation of Japanese interest rates rising to around 3%. Japan will eventually dump US government bonds to hedge against a stronger dollar, which will cause US government bond rates to spike in the future.

Therefore, the market expects Japan's 10-year government bond rate to rise to around 1%, but it could go as high as 3%. Eventually, a stronger dollar will induce a dumping of U.S. government bonds, and Japan will have to buy yen with the proceeds of these U.S. government bond sales. I think this will happen in the third or fourth quarter.

Interest rates are rising, and even though mortgage rates in the U.S. are currently in the 7% range, people say it doesn't matter because 59% of the money is financed at 3-4% fixed rates.

And even if the base rate doesn't go up, the market rate goes up because banks reflect the market rate in the interest rate they charge on loans. It mainly reflects the market rate of bank bonds.

It is reasonable to assume that the continuation of high interest rates will lead to a second round of asset market crashes in the second half of the year.

Therefore, while the U.S. is likely to cut its benchmark interest rate by around 1-2% in the near term, the BTFP and the rate cuts will force the U.S. to urgently raise rates again to tackle inflation, which has risen to around 15%.

In other words, the U.S. is likely to do what Paul Volcker did in the 1980s: cut rates sharply and then hike them sharply again in a second round. If Powell can end this 9.1% inflation rate with a rate of just 5.25%, he will have the hand of God.

I think a little bit of inflation will be more than enough to trigger a bigger upset, and we could end up with a world where the world has to tolerate 3-4% inflation for 2-3 years.

In the 1980s, the U.S. saw an 11% inflation rate in 1974, and then suddenly, in the late 1970s, prices started to rise again, hitting a frightening 13.5% in 1980.

If this inflation rate were to occur proportionally during the Powell years, the second round of inflation would be 11.2%, and the rise in interest rates would be 18.7%.

Government bonds would yield 12%. I don't like to think about it, and I'm afraid to mention it, but the math works out proportionally.

In the U.S., interest rates were 17% in December 1976, and only returned to a similar 4.13% in February 1992, 17 years later. That's a whopping 17 years to get back to normal interest rates.

Since then, the U.S. base rate has continued to decline, even reaching 0% in December 2008, before the first rate hike in March 2022.

Investors who misjudged the current situation, i.e., those who invested in government bonds first, watching the normal economic flow and the recent decline in the inflation rate, will soon start dumping them.

This will happen all over the world, and the dollar will spike again. Thus, the long-run deflation will continue until at least 2048, and the global economy will not recover until then.

Therefore, for the first time, the author believes that the world in general, and Korea in particular, should follow Japan's lead and invest in government bonds for a long time, at least until 2029.

In addition, Japan, China, the U.K., and South Korea are likely to dump U.S. government bonds to defend their currencies, which will also cause a sharp rise in U.S. government bond yields.

In this case, KBSTAR US Long Term Government Bond Futures Inverse 2X (Synthetic H) will rise sharply.

Worryingly, commercial banks in the U.S. are also heavily invested in U.S. government bonds, and BOA has a huge unrealized loss assessment. If U.S. government bonds, which are supposed to be a safe asset, are falling like this, you might wonder if government bonds of other countries around the world, including Korea, are not also unsafe assets.

In addition, countries around the world hold huge amounts of U.S. government bonds as part of their foreign exchange reserves.

The collapse in the valuation of U.S. government bonds has been driven by the FRB's continued rate hikes. Using the 10-year government bond as a baseline, a 1% increase in interest rates causes a 7% drop in government prices.

SVB's 10-year U.S. government bond would have fallen 4.75%×7%=33.25%. A 20-year U.S. government bond would have fallen in value by 4.75%×7%×2=66.5%.

Applying this principle, you can make a lot of money in a short period of time by investing in government bonds. When you expect such a sharp change in interest rates, such as a 2,100% jump from 0.25% to 5.25%, even government bonds can be a very risky asset.

In normal times, they are an absolutely safe asset, but when interest rates spike, as they are now, long-term government bonds become a risky asset.

However, it goes without saying that government bonds are

the best investment when interest rates are falling. I think
the next 40 years will be a world of high interest rates, no
inflation, and 3-4% inflation for more than a decade.

Then all asset investments will have to be reconsidered. I
think there will be a big price correction between assets. The
statistic is that after a change in interest rates, on average,
you spend 11 months at the plateau rate.

There is a very good chance that we will be in a period of
high interest rates of 7~10% and inflation rates of 3-4% for
at least two or three more years. We're already almost a year
into it. Everyone should be prepared for this.

No one will survive Higher for Longer, because interest rates
have already jumped 2100%, or 21X. It's been more than a
year since we went from 0.25% to 5.25%.

If inflation lasts much longer, the best opportunity to take
advantage of the Long Term Deflation may not come for less
than a decade. However, the author believes that this inflation
will be caught within 10 years at most.

To catch the current 9.1% inflation rate, interest rates would
have to rise to 18.7%, which is a mere math problem
compared to the Paul Volcker era. If inflation spikes to 15%,
as Bond King Gundlach says it will, the unthinkable will
happen.

Paul Volcker said that to keep inflation under control, interest
rates would have to rise sharply and then fall sharply again.
In 1980, the inflation rate jumped to 13.5% again. By

December 1980, he had to raise rates again to 22.0%. Gundlach, the bond king, had been a bond king for 40 years, so he could see this coming.

Therefore, you shouldn't rush to buy government bonds just because they cut the interest rate once in a while, hoping that this time it will be low again. As usual, if you predict the highest interest rates in advance and start investing in government bonds, you will die. The situation is coming that no one can predict.

In 1981, when Paul Volcker (August 6, 1979 – August 11, 1987) was the 12th FRB Chairman, the US interest rate was a stunning 22%. By our calculations, the final government bond rate would be 18.7% this time around.

Normally, if the government bond rate is above 6%, it is customary to get an IMF bailout. Government bonds bought at that time were locked in at that rate for 30 years.

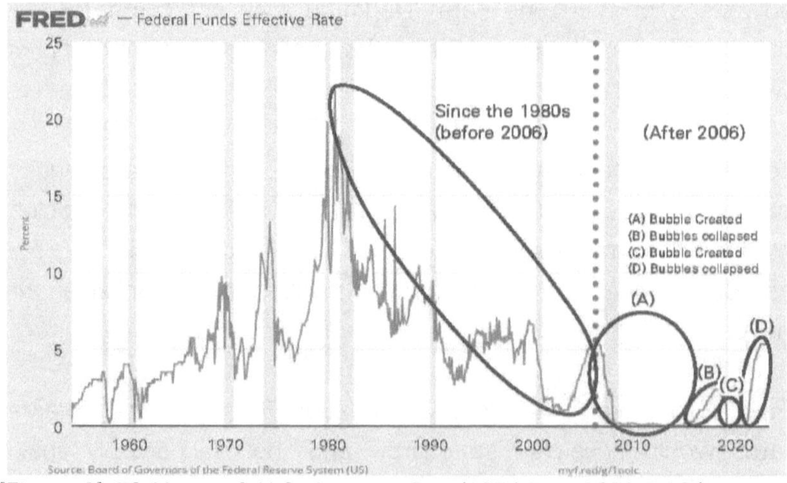

[Figure 3] 70 Years of U.S. Interest Rate(1954.7.1.–2023.5.30.)

A 15% base rate would make the Macquarie Infrastructure Fund unattractive, as its average distribution rate is around 7%. If the Macquarie Infrastructure Fund has a maturity of 20 years (2042-2023=20 years), it would be down by 14% of the market price.

If an asset yields 15% or less, i.e., less than the base rate, its price will crash. No one would be able to take on debt, such as a mortgage, because they would have to pay high interest rates for a long period of time.

Consider [Figure 3], which shows the change in the U.S. base rate over about 70 years.

Once again, the Fed will hike the base rate from 0.25% in March 2022 to 5.25% in May 2023 in a very short period of time, a 2,100% (21x) increase, and then, after the interest rate plateau, it will hastily lower rates again due to a sharp drop in the economy.

This will cause inflation to spike again. This will cause inflation to spike again, and they will raise rates sharply to keep up with inflation

After that, I think we'll have to go back to the 1980s and cut rates sharply again. This is because people's psychology is the same as it has always been. So I think Powell, like Volcker, will make a mistake this time.

Once again, we expect the Fed to raise the base rate from 0.25% in March 2022 to 5.25% in May 2023 in a very short period of time, a 2,100% (21X) increase, and then, after the interest rate plateau, to cut interest rates again in a hurry as the economy declines. This will cause inflation to rise again.

To keep inflation in check, the Fed will raise rates sharply again.
After that, we'll have to cut rates sharply again like we did in the 1980s. I think Powell will make the same mistake as Volcker did in the 1980s, because people's psychology is the same as it has always been.

After that, we could have a period of high interest rates lasting 17 to 40 years, with inflation at 3 to 4 percent for two to three years or even longer, which means inflation will be sticky, and a global inflation target of 2 percent should be seen as a virtually unrealistic goal.

A long period of high interest rates and high inflation would be transformative for asset markets. After nearly 40 years of 3-4% inflation, bank lending rates would be in the 9-10% range, and all asset prices would be due for a major correction.

It is around January-February 2023 that Korean CD rates will skyrocket, with the highest deposit rates hovering around 5%. Suddenly, the government's semi-forced margin reduction has brought deposit rates down to 4%.

This is the time to wait two years for a term deposit.
As in the 1980s, the hasty rate cuts led to a surge in inflation again, leaving one last round of sharp rate hikes and involuntary rate cuts to exhaust the economy.

At this point, Korea and the world will enter a long term deflation. After that, it will be like Japan in the early 1990s: interest rates will fall over a long period of time.

Since the reversal of the 10-year and 2-year short- and long-term interest rates has already begun, it is almost certain that the long term deflation will begin with a recession four to six months from this point.

It's also worth remembering that it took Paul Volcker only five months (March 1980 to July 1980) to cut the base rate from 19.85% to 9.93%. This was followed by a 12.07% rate hike (9.93% to 22.0%) in just six months (July 1980 to December 1980).

In 10 months, he cut rates by 9.93% and then raised them by 12.07%.

This time around, we expect Powell to raise rates again very quickly to keep up with inflation that spikes in the short term after a rate cut, only to be forced to cut rates again involuntarily and sharply when the economy cools down.

In the case of SVB and other small and medium-sized local banks, the Bank Term Funding Program (BTFP), another name for QE, is being launched to allow inflation to rise even faster.
When inflation is out of control, as it has been lately, there is a very high risk of making a "Volcker's mistake".

The Volcker mistake occurred in the early 1980s when, in the face of stagflation, then-Fed Chairman Paul Volcker raised interest rates to keep inflation in check, but then and then hastily lowered rates, causing inflation to return.

I believe this will happen again, so rather than lowering short-term interest rates, it is more realistic to increase the size of QT, targeting longer-term bonds with maturities of 10 years or more, to increase long-term interest rates.

Since January 2016, South Korea and the rest of the world have entered a long term deflation, just like Japan did in 1990. Will interest rates continue to fall in the long term like in Japan and Korea in [Figure 4] and [Figure 5]? The truth is, no one knows.The whole world is heading into the unknown

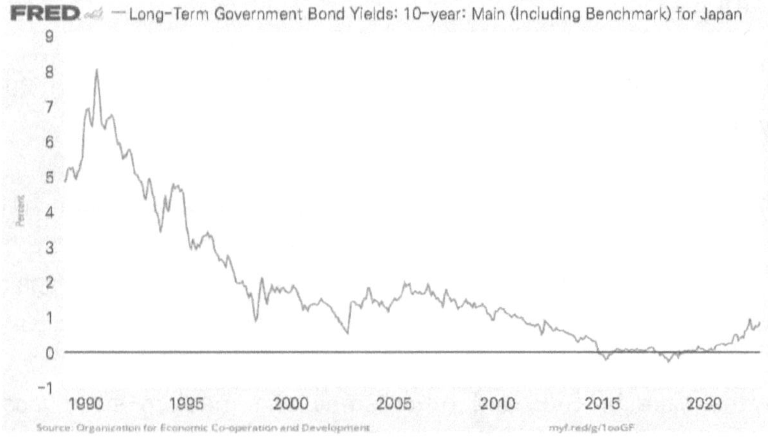

[Figure 4] Japan's 34-year (1989.1.1.~2024.4.1.) 10-year government bond rate

While global long term deflation, as measured by the relationship between the international gold price and the international dolar price, is a bit more uncertain, we believe that long term deflation in Korea is now inevitable. We have reached an environment that looks too much like Japan in early January 1990.

The amount of debt of households, corporations, and governments, the way they are repaying it, and the declining working-age population.

Add to that the fatigue of economic entities in each country due to the wild swings in the US interest rate, which is the world's base rate. These are unlikely to be resolved in the short term, which is also similar to what happened in Japan.

It is customary for any country facing an IMF crisis to be bailed out once the discount rate on its government bonds reaches 6%. The government's base rate plus a +α rate is the real interest rate. This +α includes several things.

It means that the real interest rate, which is the market rate, can go up even if the base rate doesn't. +[Figure 4] and [Figure 5] are graphs showing interest rates in Japan and South Korea during the same period.

The graph in [Figure 5] shows how interest rates in South Korea skyrocketed after the December 3, 1997 IMF crisis. At the time of the IMF, Korea's mortgage rate was a whopping 16.5%. Since 1990, interest rates in South Korea, the United States, and Japan have been on a steady decline.

In this kind of deflation, especially long term deflation, the only asset to invest in is government bonds. Of course, corporate bonds are also widely available, but in a recession, all companies cannot afford to pay the interest on their debt, and corporate profits are reduced.

This is why the author does not recommend investing in corporate bonds and only recommends government bonds as a safe haven.

In the long term, interest rates on government bonds will fall to near negative rates, and government bonds will be the only asset whose price will continue to rise.

In particular, Korea, where we believe the entry into long term deflation is most certain and strongest, does not have to take into account the nearly 40 years of high interest rates that have come to the world market – just look at Japan's lost 32 years.

Now, let's take a look at why government bond prices drop when interest rates fall, and by how much. This will help you understand how to invest in government bonds during interest rate fluctuations.

Korean government bonds have already risen once, i.e., the price of government bonds has risen preemptively in anticipation of a decrease in government bond rates, but we explained earlier that there will be one or two rate cuts and a sharp increase in interest rates and an involuntary rate cut when the plateau is passed in 2024 due to a resurgence in inflation.

With the accumulating current account deficit and the Triffin's dilemma, the crisis is likely to emerge in full force after June 2024. Eventually, the financial crisis will lead to a round of foreign dumping of Korean government bonds due to the exchange rate appreciation.

[Figure 5] South Korea's 34-year (1989.1.1.-2024.4.1) 10-year government bond rate

This is the time to buy Korean government bonds. I think we will see a sustained surge in the price of government bonds, like the 14-year period during the Great Depression in the U.S. and the lost 32 years in Japan.

The government bond bubble was briefly seen in apartment bonds during the IMF, and it will be seen again for a considerable period of time, not only in Korean government bonds but also in government bonds around the world.

The top is when everyone is shouting that bonds are the best, regardless of interest rates, and that's when government bond bubbles are most likely to burst.

Japanese interest rates crashed from 8.3% in 1990 to 0.38%

on March 27, 2015. After that, of course, it was negative, and until April 2023, it was almost the only negative rate in the world.

The rule of inertia usually comes into play when rates fall, so you should exit the bond market after the second rise. There is no reason to hurry this time. Above [Figure 6] is a long-term graph of the US 30-year mortgage rate.

As you can see, there was a long downtrend in interest rates in the US for 41 years (1981.10.-2021.1). Since interest rates have been falling for 41 years, many experts predict that interest rates will rise for the next 40 years or so.
If it does, the world turns upside down. That's why anticipating and investing ahead of time is too risky a choice. You need to see and act.

[Figure 6] US 53-year (1971,4.2-2024.5.30) 30-year US Mortgage Rates

Since Korea is 8 years into a long term deflation due to demographics, you should buy long term government bonds. When the government has cut the base interest rate at least once and is much more likely to do so again, when the dot plot is above 60%, you should buy government bonds and hold them for a long time, close to 30 years.

Due to the impact of the exchange rate surges on market sentiment, I believe that Korean government bonds will be much more undershooting compared to their intrinsic value.

*Timing is probably late 2024 to first half of 2025, I think. That's roughly one year from May 2024, when the interest rate plateau has just passed.

Usually at this time, the exchange rate surges with the financial crisis, so there is a big dumping by foreigners, which leads to a dumping of government bonds.

Government bonds, stocks, and apartments are also dumped, and prices drop to the final bottom. The stock market experiences several circuit breaks.

* Next year, after June 2025, when the dumping is completely over, will be the optimal time to invest in Korean government bonds. Of course, stocks and apartments are not yet.

Although the prices of stocks and apartments have bottomed out, they won't start to rise until the country's annual balance of payments is in surplus.

Then, when the rising exchange rate starts to calm down, foreigners now rush back into the government bond market to take advantage of the exchange rate differential.

The current situation where US government bonds are cheaper than Korean government bonds is also a sign that something is very wrong.

Then, as interest rates continue to fall, government bonds continue to rise and rise and rise, creating a bubble. After a long period of bubble formation and the collapse of the bubble in government bonds with interest rate hikes, i.e. around 2029 (Korea) to 2048 (all excluding Korea), it is time to consider selling government bonds and moving to the stock market.

A new decade of asset cycles will begin.
You have to paddle when the water is coming in.
The water comes in once every 10 years. Investing in stocks, apts, dollars now is like paddling in no-water land.
2024 This is the era of time deposits.
The age of government bonds is coming.

Because of these fluctuations in interest rates and exchange rates, government bonds are not always safe.
Even government-guaranteed bonds are not always immune to interest rate and exchange rate fluctuations.

As the bankruptcy of Silicon Valley Bank (SVB) in April 2023 and other bank failures have shown, U.S. government bonds are not always a risk-free asset, especially long-term government bonds. They are only safe if you hold them to maturity.

When interest rates rise or fall sharply, even if you don't buy or sell government bonds, the actual valuation loss or valuation gain is hidden in the bank's pocket.Even if it's a potential gain or loss, it means that the credit rating of the bank or company will be adjusted.

This will have a significant impact on the lending and interest rates of the banks and companies involved.Let's take a look at how government bond bubbles burst.

Chapter 12) Reasons for the collapse of the second government bond bubble: Scenarios ① ②③

Contrary to what people expect and think, the current interest rate environment is split between those who think rates are headed higher for longer and those who think they are not.

In other words, there is a split between those who believe that inflation will remain at 3-4% for more than a decade and those who believe that the Fed will start lowering rates as soon as this year.

The author considers all three scenarios, and believes that you should invest in government bonds to prepare for them.In other words, there are three possible future scenarios.

In all three scenarios, there is no way to avoid a secondary burst of the government bond bubble.Let's start with the first scenario, which is more likely.

(1) Scenario①
Jerome Powell, in response to public expectations, cuts rates early, triggering a second round of inflation, meaning that the early rate cut forces the world to raise interest rates dramatically to get inflation under control again.
This is Paul Volcker's mistake.

Like Paul Volcker's mistake, we could see Jerome Powell's

mistake. I think this is much more likely. It is important to realize that historical interest rate hikes to control inflation usually take three waves before they are over.
[Figure 3] Let's look again at the graph of the US interest rate over 70 years (1954.7.1. to 2023.5.30.).

Looking at [Figure 3], we have been through a period of high interest rates for about 40 years, followed by a tunnel of low interest rates for about 40 years. The question is whether we are now entering a period of high interest rates again.

It is true that during this period, China joined the WTO on December 11, 2001, and the world has experienced inflation-free economic growth for more than two decades.

Then, due to the coronavirus, the US and China again imposed trade restrictions on each other, raising the price of all commodities.

This is probably the main reason why the world is facing inflation again.
In response to this inflation, the U.S. has responded by sharply raising its base rate by 2100% (21 x) in a short period of time. The Fed raised interest rates by 0.25% to 5.25%, but inflation hasn't caught up.

Since interest rates have risen so rapidly in a short period of time, households, businesses, governments, and other economic entities are anxiously awaiting a rate cut. In addition, the 2024 U.S. presidential election is on November 5, so politics may also play a role.

Jerome Powell, the sixth chairman of the U.S. Federal Reserve, may get caught up in impatience and market sentiment and cut rates too quickly. Politics could also be a factor in premature rate cuts and errors in judgment. In November, there is a US presidential election. If this happens, inflation could spike again, forcing the Fed to raise rates again.

This will cause the economy to sharply decline, and then the economy will crash, forcing the Fed to cut rates again. This is the 'Powell mistake'. Powell will make the same mistake as former Federal Reserve Chairman Paul Volcker. From this point, a long, long deflationary period will begin in earnest.

(2) Scenario②
Contrary to popular expectations, if interest rates stay high for longer, any economic entity will be unable to pay its debts and go bankrupt. No economic entity can survive 2-3 years with interest rates spiking 2100%.

Any economic entity has too much debt, and once it collapses, it will fall like dominoes, resulting in a financial crisis-style recession. In response, foreign funds will rush out of the country to avoid exchange losses. As a result, the dollar's exchange rate surges.

As a result, the dollar exchange rate surges, causing foreign investors to dump government bonds and stocks. The price of government bonds, stocks, and apartments crashes.

The government eventually responds by cutting interest rates. Similarly, in Scenario 2, a bubble burst is inevitable as foreigners dump government bonds and stocks.

After that, we believe that the bubble will burst in earnest with long term deflation. Long term deflation will continue to lower interest rates, which will lead to a steady increase in government bond prices.

3)Scenario ③.
Coincidentally, South Korea will launch a financial investment tax in 2025. It is said that about 150 trillion won will leave the domestic market at this time.

First, in order to avoid the financial investment tax, rich Koreans who have a lot of financial assets will sell financial assets such as government bonds and stocks to avoid the tax, and the dollar will surge when converting these funds into dollars to take them out of the country.

Foreign funds will also naturally sell domestic stocks and government bonds to avoid exchange losses. This is the best opportunity to invest in government bonds in a lifetime.

If you buy government bonds after the market crashes, the price difference at that time is already embedded in the purchase price of government bonds, so you can enjoy the price difference and interest until maturity. This is why you shouldn't try to anticipate and invest in government bonds ahead of time. There's never been a better time to buy.

(Conclusion 1)
The future direction of the Fed's base rate is one of scenarios ①, ②, or ③.

In the case of ①, due to Powell's sudden interest rate cut, the price of government bonds skyrockets -> secondary inflation occurs again due to the interest rate cut -> interest rates are inevitably raised to calm inflation again -> a secondary crash in government bond prices appears -> a long term deflationary spiral begins -> a long period of interest rate cuts awaits.

In our view, one interest rate cut and one interest rate hike remain in the future. There is a 70% probability of ①.

In the case of ②, Koreans who cannot withstand high interest rates for a long time will sell government bonds and stock ,apartments, causing prices to crash. According to the diamond dollar investment method, the dollar soars.

Eventually, foreigners will also sell to avoid exchange losses, causing a major collapse in domestic assets such as government bonds, stocks, and apartments. Even in this case, after the crash, a long boom awaits due to interest rate cuts. It has about a 30% probability.

In the case of scenario ③, the enforcement date has already been set for early next year. It is a certainty. The probability of such a phenomenon is more than 80%.

In all three cases, investing in government bonds is the perfect jackpot. You will have the opportunity to enjoy a long term decline in interest rates and a continuous rise in government bond prices.

In all three scenarios, the gains and losses are already built into the price of the bonds, so holding them to maturity will allow you to take advantage of all the gains. For buyers, this is the best time to buy.

After you buy, you'll still realize additional gains from falling interest rates, but it's up to you to decide whether you want to sell midstream or hold the bond to maturity and take advantage of the existing gains.

Japan has been in long term deflation for 32 years and the US for 19 years. South Korea won't exit long term deflation until 2029, and the world won't exit long term deflation until 2048. Until then, you can enjoy the rising price of government bonds that earn interest every year.

The bubble, which was inflated with money released during the long period of interest rate cuts due to the financial crisis and the coronavirus, must now be reevaluated.

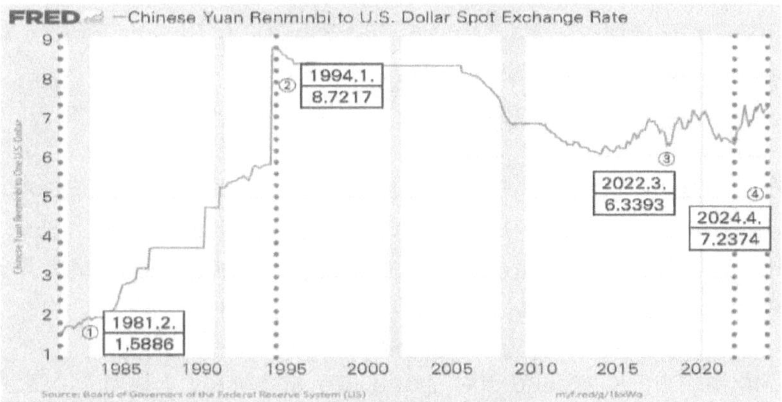

[Figure 7] China's exchange rate changes

In other words, there will be individuals and companies that will fail as the secondary bubble bursts, triggered by premature interest rate cuts. There will also be banks and savings banks that will fail.

In other words, the secondary government bond bubble is destined to burst because of premature interest rate cuts.

When this bubble bursts, the dollar rises sharply and government bonds drop as foreign money flows out of the country. The government is then forced to cut interest rates again, and a long period of deflation ensues.

As shown in the graph of ultra-long-term Japanese interest rates in Figure 2, the base rate will continue to fall indefinitely, creating a reverse bubble in government bond prices. In the long term, we expect interest rates to drop to near negative rates again, similar to Japan.

(Conclusion 2)
With the U.S. base rate having jumped as much as 5%, regional banks in the U.S. should be recording huge valuation losses. Allen's actions delayed the write-downs until May, but the deferral is now over.

Central banks around the world are also facing huge losses because they've filled their reserves with U.S. government bonds, meaning that every country is running out of reserves.

Interest rates set the price of everything in the world, and when interest rates rise, so do exchange rates. Each asset has a traditional rate of return, which is based on the interest rate.

This means that if interest rates go up, the rent of an apartment won't be the same as it was before interest rates went up.

In other words, if the yields of stocks, apartments, and offices, which are typical financial assets, differ from each other, the funds will be moved to the assets with higher yields in the medium to long term, and the yields of all assets will be similar in the long run.

This is evidence that interest rates are the "invisible hand". In this case, interest rates jumped 21 x (2100%) in a short period of time.

Eventually, there will be a secondary bubble burst in government bonds, which is expected to be triggered by scenarios ①, ②, and ③. Therefore, knowing how to invest in the case of a government bond bubble burst is too good to be true for future investments.

Finally,
The outcome of the U.S. presidential election will also be a factor that will affect the bursting of the bond bubble. After the TV debate,

Trump's chances of re-election are increasing, and his economic policies are expected to cause a rise in the inflation rate.

This is because the imposition of high tariffs on Chinese products and the imposition of tariffs on all products from friendly countries is expected to trigger inflation. This is likely to trigger a second round of interest rate hikes to calm inflation.

The subsequent increase in inflation is expected to cause a sharp rise in interest rates, which may become Scenario ④ among the factors for the secondary collapse of the government bond bubble. The current period can be described as an era of chaos.

Chapter 13)How to Invest When the Government Bond Bubble Bursts

When the bubble bursts, as it did in Venezuela, Argentina, and other countries in southern Europe, the domestic dollar of the country soars. Foreigners, especially U.S. funds invested in the crisis countries, should quickly sell and convert their bonds back to their home country's currency to mitigate their losses.

Non-Americans return home, sell their dollars, and exchange them for their home currency, causing the value of their currency to skyrocket. If you take Japan as an example, you can see that the yen has risen sharply and the dollar has fallen sharply. This phenomenon is known as the "Japanese curse".

When foreign investment assets are dumped over a short period of time, the dollar price plummets when foreigners withdraw. The IMF situation in Korea is an example of this. Naturally, the time for the dollar to calm down depends on the severity of the crisis and the country.

1) Buy government bonds that foreigners are dumping.

Government bonds and stock, apartments that foreigners are selling to avoid currency losses are the things to buy. They will rise sharply when the crisis subsides. It is a temporary drop due to selling to avoid exchange losses rather than selling due

to a change in the safety of the bond.
In a long term deflation, only government bonds can continue to rise in price due to continued interest rate cuts. Stocks and apartments will fall 80–90% by the end of the deflation period.

2) Buy an eligible inverse

On the other hand, various inverse products are good investment targets.
 –KODEX 200 Futures Inverse 2X and government bond inverse ETFs are also alternatives.
 –The KBSTAR US Long Term Government Bond Futures Inverse 2X(Synthetic H)is a temporarily effective countermeasure.

If US interest rates rise, the 10–year government bond will increase by 7% per 1%. Since this product is 2X, it will increase by 14%.

3) Buy stock in the Macquarie Infrastructure Fund.
Macquarie Infrastructure The Macquarie Infrastructure Fund, available only in Korea, is a financial product that combines stock and fund functions.

It is a product called Macquarie Infrastructure (code number: 088980) that invests in social indirect capital in Korea and gives dividends of 675~900 won every year. It is created and managed by Macquarie Bank of Australia.

It is a time–limited fund that will be dissolved in 2043. It pays much higher dividends than government bonds, and because

of its international reputation, it is a kind of real estate REIT that cannot break its dividend promises.
This stock is MRG, which has a guaranteed minimum yield.

The Korean government guarantees the yield. It's like a government bond in that it has an inverse relationship with interest rates, although it's possible that it could be underutilized due to deflation and only receive the minimum yield.

However, to put it in perspective, Macquarie Infrastructure is like a government bond with a duration of 2042-2024 = about 19 years.

The annual dividend is expected to be 675 to 900 won per year starting in 2018. That's about a 7% annualized return on your investment. Although the government has guaranteed a minimum return with MRGs, the expected dividend amount in the event of a minimum return is not known.

In other words, the expected dividend amount (675 won to 900 won) is not the minimum expected dividend, but the expected dividend amount assuming that the profit will gradually increase as it is now.

The difference with government bonds is that they do not return the face value of 5,000 won (issue price 7,000 won) at maturity, but are forced to make three installments before maturity.

Starting in 2023, the expected dividend is more than 700 won per year, so the total amount of distributions is 700 won × 20 years = 14,000 won.

This is a way to hedge against the Macquarie Infrastructure Fund's price fluctuations before investing. If there is an era of high interest rates in the future, the Macquarie Infrastructure Fund will not be immune to a price crash.

However, if you hold to maturity, you will never lose more than the purchase price through distributions (dividends) alone.

You should also consider that the principal of $5,000 will be returned in three installments. In 2024, that is, this year, a portion of the 5,000 won face value, 1,300 won, will be refunded.

Inflation is expected to remain at 4–5% for the next two to three years, and high interest rates are likely to come. Macquarie Infrastructure Fund is a better investment than government bonds

4)Gold and Bitcoin are not investments at all.
1) Gold will crash
- While some people predict a rise in the price of gold, gold is almost completely illiquid and is not an asset that foreigners should invest in when selling domestic assets to avoid currency losses.

Gold is not a good investment at all, as it will soon be followed by a long term deflation. Gold is still about 60% overvalued compared to other assets.

2) Bitcoin disappears like smoke, i.e., it's not Bitcoin

Bitcoin is no longer an asset class. On January 10, 2024 (local time), the Bitcoin Physical ETF was listed on the U.S. stock market, which means that Bitcoin is no longer mysterious and secretive anymore.

It is subject to strict ownership-transfer controls by the SEC in each country.
Just as the Swiss banks have given up their secrecy, Bitcoin is now destined to disappear overnight.

Chapter 14)The Ghost Dollar is Born

No one knows the exact amount, but somewhere between $6 and $10 trillion or more is currently floating around the international financial markets like a ghost with no destination.

The largest portion of this money is invested by Japanese citizens in overseas stocks, bonds, and profitable real estate. Because of potential exchange rate losses due to the strong yen, about $3.5 trillion has been floating around abroad for more than 40 years without being brought back into Japan. Now, with a sustained lower yen, some of it may be coming back.

Next, the overseas operating profits of U.S. tech companies such as Apple and Microsoft, which cannot be brought back to the U.S. to avoid taxes, have also become ghost dollars. These large funds are floating around in offshore financial firms without a destination.

The author designates these funds as ghost dollars. In a nutshell, ghost dollar refers to a tramp dollar that does not return to its home country to avoid incurring losses such as exchange losses and taxes when returning to its home country and wanders aimlessly in the international financial market.

Ghost dollars are dollars that were invested abroad or legitimate money earned from overseas business, but when they return home, they cannot return home due to huge exchange rate losses or taxes, and are wandering the world. This is what ghost dollars are.

These dollars are ghost dollars and wandering dollars because they cannot return home. (wandering dollar) and becomes a homeless dollar.

This money is completely different in nature and origin than hot money. Hot money is dollar funds that move between countries in a short period of time in pursuit of speculative gains.

Hot money is a nuisance to the international economy, causing many countries to rush to introduce Tobin taxes on hot money as it crosses their borders, and it can also be decisively harmful to countries with weak foreign exchange reserves.

Rather than operating according to economic principles, these are funds that enter when a country is in crisis, take advantage of short-term gains, and then exit. This is why the capital account is more important than the current account, which affects domestic asset markets such as stocks, real estate, and government bonds.

On the other hand, most ghost dollars are well-motivated and benign in nature. According to Bloomberg, tech companies like Apple, Microsoft, and Alphabet hold $2.6 trillion in cash overseas.

These are legitimate funds earned from doing business abroad. This money is taxed at about 35% the moment it is brought into the US. US President Donald Trump has promised to reduce this tax to 10% in his campaign.

So, sooner or later, these U.S. companies' foreign earnings will stop being phantom dollars. It's just a matter of reconciling tax rates.

The ghost dollars of U.S. tech companies are different from the ghost dollars of Japanese overseas investment failures. Japan is the world's largest creditor nation, with over $10 trillion in overseas investments and $3.5 trillion in net worth abroad. Of this $10 trillion, nearly 50%, or $4.53 trillion, is invested in stocks and other securities.

Subtracting an estimated $1.3 trillion in local loans, $3.5 trillion of the overseas net worth has become phantom dollars that have been floating around for more than 40 years.

In other words, the largest amount of ghost money floating

around internationally is the money that Japanese people have failed to invest abroad and are scheduled to suffer huge exchange losses when they bring it home.

As explained in [Chapter 3], even though Abenomics policies have recovered about 49% of these funds, there is still a 26% loss in the valuation of overseas investments, so the public has been unable to bring their wealth home for more than 40 years.

The author predicts that the won will continue to strengthen in the future, and almost all of these funds are destined to become ghost dollars, if not already. In the author's view, the bottom for the won is well below 760 won.

The reason for this is easy to see by comparing it to Japan's long term deflation. As in Japan, the difference will be so great that it will be unspeakable.

While the above examples of ghost dollars are legitimate, ghost dollars can also include illegal funds such as tax evasion hidden offshore or in tax havens.

These ghost dollars do not yet have a negative effect on the global economy or the countries in which they are hidden. Almost all of the Japanese money is invested in the U.S., with another 30% or so spread across Europe and elsewhere. Of course, there is also a mix of M&A funds from the acquisition of overseas companies.

Having a lot of foreign net worth isn't always a good thing. Large overseas assets can also be a weakness: the value of Japanese people's assets is directly affected by economic and currency fluctuations overseas.

This also affects the domestic economy.
It is important to realize that these ghost dollars have been benign so far, but their behavior may change in the future.

Compared to when the dollar was expensive in the 1970s, when it peaked at 360 yen, the yen is already scheduled to lose about 56% of its value even at 160 yen today.

Foreign net worth is the amount of a country's income or wealth that is not spent domestically, but instead goes abroad. It's no wonder that Japan's domestic economy would be depressed. It is one of the main causes of Japan's chronic economic stagnation, or the 32 lost years.

Paradoxically,
it could be argued that Japan's accumulated trade surplus has actually created the country's chronic recession.This is because the growing trade surplus has allowed income to flow out of the country and abroad, withholding domestic consumption, for decades.

The income, or wealth, of Japanese people abroad is roughly twice the size of Japan's gross domestic product (GDP) in a year.

That's about two years' worth of their entire income that they don't even spend.

Chapter 15) A concrete example of a jackpot during the bond bubble burst

In Korea, the era of private investment in government bonds has come to an end, and government bond investment has boomed, and government bonds have begun to bubble in earnest.

Naturally, the middle class participates in this government bond investment boom. This government bond bubble soon collapses along with the middle class. Therefore, it's a good idea to analyze in advance how to get richer when the bond bubble bursts, through specific examples.

How to properly invest in government bonds that no one has ever explained before!
I will introduce concrete examples and the conditions for hitting the jackpot.

(1) Reconstruction Ministry bonds and Vietnam, etc.

In the early stages of economic development, any country often raises industrial capital by attaching government bonds to various license applications and forcibly digesting them.

The government bonds issued at this time were mainly used as paper for children to make scabs. I remember folding these bonds and playing with them.

At the time, few people predicted that Korea would be able to repay the bonds and the interest, so adults didn't stop them. The owner of the now-defunct Youngdong Development Promotion Center, who secretly bought them for a little more than the price of toilet paper and stored them in a warehouse.

Later, the Korean government, with its improved finances, paid all the principal and interest on the government bonds in cash, contrary to popular belief. In today's money, it would have been worth hundreds of billions of won.

Vietnam, China, North Korea, Laos, etc. may have government bonds that have been issued and forcibly digested for such development policies, so you should keep a close eye on them.Jackpot opportunities may be hidden.

As mentioned above, the founder of the construction company Youngdong Development & Promotion is the one who won a historic jackpot by investing in bonds.

She probably made hundreds of billions at current prices. She collected a lot of reconstruction bonds in her warehouse. At that time, Korea didn't even have the technology to make stiff paper.

The face value was completely disregarded and collected by junkman with scales. It is believed that they acted as middlemen for the junkman or moneylender. I know, because

I was seduced by junkman and I traded Japanese bonds for yeot behind my father's back.

(2) There's a huge opportunity in North Korean government bonds.

Currently, North Korea cannot issue government bonds to raise new funds in international capital markets. However, there are North Korean government bonds that have been issued and defaulted on international markets in the past.

These are traded in the United States and are known to trade at around 3-4% of their face value. If the country were to reunify one day, it would probably be paid off by South Korea. It would be a jackpot bond.

(3) Success story of the founder of Mirae Asset Securities at the time of the IMF

It was the founder of Mirae Asset who really hit the jackpot with bonds after the IMF crisis broke out. In early 1998, when market interest rates were hitting 30% per annum, he made a $20 billion pooled bet on bonds, which I understand was borrowed money. If he had invested in stocks at that time, he would have been completely ruined.

When market interest rates dropped to 20% in March of the same year, bond prices, of course, skyrocketed. If he had bet on 10-year government bonds, they would have gone up 10×7=70% in price, making him about 14 billion in three months. This profit is net profit without any taxes. This is what fintech, or financial technology, is all about.

You shouldn't full bet on stocks or real estate.
Gap investing in apartments or margin trading, or trading stocks on credit, are both risky. However, you can pool bet on government bonds. Government bonds are safer than bank deposits because they are guaranteed by the government, but only up to $50 million per bank.

The key to investing is not the rate of return, but how much you can invest. Buying government bonds is actually like making a deposit with the government. Long-term government bonds are sensitive to interest rates, but if you hold them to maturity, they are an absolutely safe asset.

The author believes that this opportunity, which Park Hyun-joo has taken advantage of, will come around the first half of 2026. After that, another long term deflation awaits us.

To summarize, government bond prices are due for one more crash along with the dollar's surge, followed by a long period of rising prices. There are two big opportunities left for the Korean middle class and Korean investors.

(4)Hit the jackpot with BW

Mr. ○○○, the owner of the now defunct Sejong Securities (now NH Investment & Securities), once made dozens of times the profit with BW (Bond with Warrant). The author also studied this case and earned 16x profit in about 6 months with WR.

I once invested 18 million won in Sejong Securities' warrant bonds and gained up to 600 million won in a short period of time, up to 33.3 times, the highest capital gain in my life.

This was about 15 years ago. However, the author missed the right time to sell due to greed and had to settle for 16.6x, i.e, 300 million won, which greatly reduced his profit.

Since then, the author has been using the three-line break to find the right time to sell. When it comes to identifying when to buy, he only uses the three-line conversion chart as a secondary confirmation.

The disadvantage of the Three line break is that if the amount of ups and downs is too large, it will be too late to sell or buy when you see that the line has changed to a negative or positive line.

Therefore, after this accident(?), I modified and applied my own unique investment technique of the Three Line break, which is to sell unconditionally when the price drops 10% from the highest price.

Anyway, the big money is made by investing in bonds. Among them, especially government bonds are 100% safe, so you can make full betting. The key to investing is not the yield, but how much you can concentrate your investments. Government bonds are safer than bank CDs.

Even banks only guarantee payment up to 50 million won. Like the jackpot example above, you should study bonds in advance, especially government bonds, so that when it's your turn to win, you don't miss out.

Bonds are the perfect golden cushion for those who are prepared and knowledgeable. Readers of this book will recognize this already.

As shown in [Figure 8], first of all, as we saw in the U.S. in 1929 and Japan's Lost 32 Years, in a long-term deflation, interest rates continue to fall in a recession, causing bond prices to skyrocket.

In addition, government bonds pay 2-3% in interest annually, and more importantly, in the long term deflation, interest rates will continue to fall for about 30 years, which will lead to a massive increase in the price of government bonds. This is a huge bull market for government bonds.

Government bonds and the Macquarie Infrastructure Fund are must-have assets in the final five steps of the Pentagon's investment method.

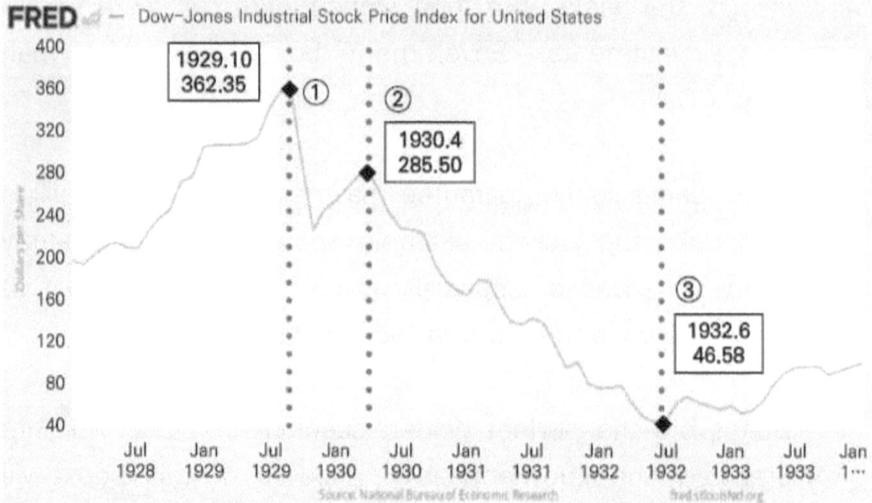

[Figure 8] US Dow

Look at the collapse of Japanese interest rates over a long period of 32 years of deflation [Figure 4]! Japanese government bonds are so expensive that their value is incalculable.

The fact that they are such a good financial product that no one is selling them is proof of this. So they don't even have a price. Since 2016, the world has been in a long term deflation. Let's not forget that since 2016, the world has been in a long term deflation!

(5) Apartment bonds

Something similar happened in the 1980s, which the author experienced firsthand.

In order to recoup the difference between the sale price and the market price of apartments, the government forced people to buy national housing bonds and locked in the profits for 20 years.

At the time, the discounted market price of a 100-million-won bond with a face value of 100 million won was around 9 million won. When my first child graduated from elementary school, I decided to buy the bonds, but I didn't have enough money at the time.

If I had only bought 9 million won, or 100 million won, at the time, I would have received about 81 million won in interest over 20 years at 3% interest and 20 years of compounding. Of course, I would have gotten back the original 100 million won. I missed a big opportunity of a lifetime.

Because it was a 20-year bond, it was also exempt from inheritance tax. They don't even issue them anymore. After the IMF, the bond traded at a premium, meaning that the face value of the bond was 100 million won plus future interest, plus a premium.

Predicting the future situation like this, the opportunity to become rich comes every once in a while, so you should study finance on a regular basis so that you can seize this opportunity.

In hindsight, this is the complete opposite of what the experts predicted at the time. It was a reversal of the vague predictions of experts and the general public that inflation would turn bonds into toilet paper.

(5) The author does not recommend municipal bonds, corporate bonds, or perpetual bonds.

In times of crisis, corporate bonds usually trade at around 20% of their face value, but they rarely recover, and you'll be difficult to find 20% after distributing the remaining assets.

If a company has any remaining assets, the first thing it must do is pay off its debenture holders. These debentures are always prioritized over stock. After distributing the property to the debenture holders, the stockholders can only get a share of the property if there is any residual property.

But there's something else I learned from the collapse of Credit Suisse. It gave a concrete application of the contingent convertible bond (CoCobond). CoCobonds are corporate bonds with a condition that the bond can be forcibly converted into shares or canceled for free in the event of an emergency.

Although it pays a little more interest, perpetual bonds, which have been issued by quite a few large Korean companies, should also be reviewed in detail in advance. I think there will be specific application cases in Korea soon.

That's why I said not to invest in corporate bonds that are not government bonds issued by the government, but always invest in government bonds. However, you should always study these government bonds to see if there are any tricks, and you should also carefully analyze the conditions of the issuance of private government bonds this time.

As you can see, other people's crises are often great opportunities for you. Of course, if you are not prepared in advance, you will also be in a crisis.

If Korea faces another major crisis like the IMF crisis, it would be a great opportunity to invest in Korean assets by borrowing money from China or the United States, where interest rates are relatively lower than in Korea.

Since the IMF crisis was only in Korea, the interest rate difference between the U.S., China, and Japan will be lower, and Korea, which is in crisis, will have another 18% interest rate, so if you borrow from other countries or from relatives in other countries and put your money in a bank in Korea, you will earn about 15% interest, assuming no currency exchange costs.

If there is a crisis in your country, you have to look both internationally and domestically because it is the era of internationalization.

Also, one day North Korea will be absorbed and reunified with

South Korea, and that day will come without anyone realizing it. South Korea will collect huge taxes to fund North Korea's development, and international financial organizations will finance the rest of the development. It will take a lot of dollars, and it will be inflationary, so the value of the dollar will skyrocket.

It will be a great opportunity to accumulate dollars in preparation for this, or to import dollars from the United States and China immediately after reunification.

The world, including Korea, has been in Long Term Deflation since January 2016, so investing in the dollar should only be done under normal economic conditions, that is, in Short Term Deflation. However, in the event of a crisis, we can only think in the short term.

(6)However, the recent U.S. reshoring policy is a strong, long-term bullish factor for the dollar. There is also a strong and long-lasting dollar depreciation factor in the rest of the world, which arrived in January 2016.

The future direction of the dollar will be determined by the strength of the U.S. reshoring and the strength of the long-run deflationary forces in each country.

In the old days of development economies, governments borrowed a lot of cheap money from abroad in the name of borrowing, and the cheap money was given to the chaebols (today's conglomerates) at below-market interest rates.

At the time, Korea was in a chronic inflationary economy, so the difference in interest rates alone meant that the chaebols swallowed up hundreds of billions of dollars a year.

So, the world of tens of billions of dollars in political donations went on for decades without the government having to tell the chaebol to give them money.

The frequent introduction of borrowing is something that happened when I was in high school and college, but I thought at the time that borrowing was good for Korea and its people. The media was so proud of it. So we should always study economics.

The government is another thing, and it may deceive the people again in the future. There is always a big whirlwind, a social issue,

through newspaper broadcasts and so on, you must understand the new things. After a while, all the knowledge and information will converge and take over your head.

Speaking of reunification with North Korea, let me add one more thing.If reunification happens, which assets should we invest in?

You should study Germany.

It's pretty obvious that the dollar will go up.
Germany recognized the ownership of all East German land as long as there was a trace in the registry.
We will do the same.

Social indirect capital stocks will explode. KEPCO, construction, banks, etc. would have to be quickly revitalized with government funds. Global investor Jim Rogers has publicly stated that he is targeting Korean real estate and other assets at the time of reunification.

He sees it as the greatest investment opportunity in history. He is right. But giving this speculative capital a chance to invest should be done after all the facts are in.

Chapter 16) Secrets to Getting Rich Investing in Bonds (government bonds)

The examples in the previous chapter are all examples of people who took advantage of a crisis and made a fortune. If you don't study and research these opportunities on a regular basis, you won't be able to make the most of them when they come along.

The secret to getting rich investing in bonds (government bonds) is surprisingly simple

Let's take a look at them!
1) First, you need to buy government bonds cheaper than the market price.The best time to buy below the market price is when there is a crisis.

When a country faces a financial crisis or economic crisis and the exchange rate soars, foreigners will dump government bonds irrationally. This is because foreigners have to avoid both exchange losses and trading losses at the same time. This is the only time we can buy government bonds cheaper than the market price.

In other words, when foreigners are selling at dumping prices, domestic investors should buy government bonds in one-third increments. No one can time the market optimally, so you have to react by buying in splits.

2) Sell when it's most expensive
Once the crisis subsides, foreigners will start buying government bonds again. As the popularity of foreigners in investing in government bonds skyrockets, domestic investors will follow them and buy government bonds, thus re-inflating the bubble.

This is the optimal time to sell short-term government bonds. Again, no one can time the peak of the bubble, so sell in thirds. However, in this case, you need to carefully decide when to sell, taking into account points 5) and 6).

This time, you should carefully decide whether to hold long or short term, as it will lead to long term deflation.

3) Only invest in government bonds
Government bonds are bonds that are issued by the government and cannot be delayed in paying principal or interest even for a day. As good as they are, as we've explained many times before, you shouldn't invest in any bonds during normal times, let alone government bonds.

This is because the interest on government bonds is always lower than the rate of inflation, and the price of government bonds rarely fluctuates during normal times, which means that there are many other investments that have higher yields than government bonds during normal times.

4) Never invest in bonds other than government bonds,

especially during financial crises and foreign exchange crises. As I have already explained, everyone needs money in times of crisis.

Remember that even municipal bonds are unreliable in times of crisis, especially corporate bonds, as there is always a chance that they will default or suspend payments and you will lose a lot of money. However, government bonds never miss a single day of principal or interest payments.

Therefore, invest only in government bonds as they are the safest bonds, but only in times of crisis, such as financial or economic crises. In particular, you should not invest in corporate bonds under any circumstances.

5) Don't buy government bonds in the middle of a market crash, but after it is over, so that you can enjoy all the capital gains and interest rates until maturity.

In other words, if you buy government bonds at a price that reflects the market price and hold them until maturity, you can enjoy all the capital gains and interest rates.

If you buy government bonds at such an advantageous price, it is even more advantageous to hold them until maturity, even if the bubble bursts again.

As in the previous example, in the 1980s, the U.S. paid 22% interest on government bonds every year for about 30 years. That's 30 years of the unthinkable.

6) In this case, the best time to invest in government bonds is during long term deflation. This is when interest rates are expected to fall for a long period of time, and there is a very good chance that they will fall to near negative rates.

It has been explained many times that when interest rates fall, government bond prices rise sharply in response. Long-term deflation therefore represents almost the only and best opportunity for long-term high returns in government bonds.

To take advantage of these opportunities, you need to understand how bond prices work.
You need to know the difference between short-term and long-term deflation and how interest rates have changed in the past.

Understand the wisdom of the Japanese people, who have been saving steadily even when deposits pay 0% interest. They have been storing cash in cabinets and closets for a long time. This was because deposits in banks earned very little interest.

It's important to understand the wisdom of the Japanese, who have consistently saved even when deposits were paying 0% interest. This is because in a long-term deflation, the relative value of deposits (i.e cash) kept increasing because the price of other goods kept decreasing even though there was no interest.

In deflation, you shouldn't be focused on nominal interest rates. Since 2016, the world has been in a state of long term deflation.

In Korea, during the Park Chung-hee regime, which was a development economy, bank interest rates were high, so people were eager to save in banks because the interest rate was in double digits, but not many people realized that the real interest rate was negative. This is why it's important to build financial knowledge.

Another thing to know is that in a long term deflation, investing in government bonds is a more perfect jackpot than saving, because everything else goes down.

Consider the 34-year (1989.1.1-2023.5.30) ultra-long term Japanese interest rate graph in [Figure 4]. One graph proves that long term bonds are favorable in a long term deflation. How much would have been the price differential?

For the Korean KOSPI market
After a short period of surging and crashing dollar prices in June 2021, when the main bull market in the Korean stock market came to a stop, it is now the time to invest in term deposits in the second half of 2024.

If you have already invested in government bonds, due to the premature recommendation of some experts or the misjudgment of investors, you will already be in a state of huge valuation loss, that is, the first bubble has already burst.

We are now past the interest rate plateau (a period of

neither raising nor lowering rates any further and reviewing the effectiveness of the actions already taken), which lasts about 11 months on average. As of now, March 23, 2023 is the last interest rate hike date.

However, if they cut rates before they have time to see the policy effects of the rate hikes, the inflation rate will spike again.The author has previously predicted that eventually, after one or two rate cuts, they will have to raise rates again to calm inflation.

This is Scenario ① of the reasons for the collapse of the second government bond bubble in [Chapter 12]. At this point, the sharp interest rate hike causes government bonds to collapse again.

The economy then declines sharply and long- term deflation begins in earnest, and from this point on, a long period of interest rate cuts due to long- term deflation begins.

Therefore, when foreigners buy back the government bonds they have sold, they do not need to sell the bonds they have bought, as described in paragraph 2) of Chapter 16, This time, in particular, it is because the long term deflation that awaits us is a continuous government bond price spike.

This is the most important secret to getting rich investing in bonds!

Since 2016, the world has been experiencing a long period of deflation, which is already in full swing, and this is the perfect time to invest in government bonds.

In Japan, interest rates have been falling continuously for more than 30 years, even to negative rates. This time around, the world outside of Japan will experience the same phenomenon.

In a normal recession
After the bubble burst, the government will have to lower interest rates again to stimulate the economy. After about two rounds of interest rate cuts, it's time to close time deposits and start investing in government bonds. After two or three years of investing in government bonds, the 10-year cycle will be over.

In the case of a short-term deflation, i,e a normal recession, this completes the Korean proverb that says that in 10 years, the mountains change.

This means that after 10 years, a river becomes a mountain, and a mountain becomes a river. Anyone who stays invested in one asset for a long period of time without following the flow of the asset market and rotating between assets (Asset

Cycle Investing) will suffer the consequences of the river turning into a mountain, and vice versa.

This is the Pentagon Investing Method. This is the deep meaning of Korea's ancestors' proverb. Anyone who doesn't follow this proverb will suffer great losses.

After all, money cycles through stocks, apartments, dollars, deposits, and government bonds in search of more profits, and long term investors are almost always wiped out.

Which brings us back to the bulls,
The last big winners in this asset market cycle are government bonds, Macquarie Infrastructure, KODEX 200 Inverse, and KODEX 200 Inverse Leveraged.

I believe these assets are in a major bull market until around 2048. After that, there is a very real possibility that interest rates will be lowered once or twice by impatient policymakers. Then, to combat soaring inflation, rates will rise sharply again.

This will be followed by a severe recession, or long term deflation, which will continue to push interest rates lower. This coincides with Japan's long period of interest rate cuts. [Figure 4] Japan's 10-year government bond rate over 34 years (1989.1.1. to 2024.4.1.)! Similarly, we estimate that Korea's government bonds will rise by 2029.

No matter how much Korea wants to avoid a deflationary

economy, it will not be able to avoid the population cliff that started in 2017 and the debt problems of the country, companies, and individuals, so the deflationary economy will continue.

In the future, Korea will be as irrelevant to global economic trends as Japan. Korea is in the same situation as Japan in 1989, and Korea shouldn't forget that we already entered a deflationary economy in 2016.

Korea has never had a boom in government bonds. So, of course, there has never been a government bond bubble. However, this time, the first bubble has already burst because the U.S. raised interest rates several times and we also raised interest rates. A bubble is a word used when something is trading at a more inflated price than its actual value.

For a government bond to be in a bubble, it must be trading at a price higher than its actual earnings value. A bubble exists when government bonds trade at a premium.

Right now, there is a huge bubble in Japanese government bonds, and for more than 30 years, Japanese government bonds have been on a bullish run.

No one is selling, so there's no price, and there's nothing to buy. Korea is destined to do the same. In the United States, there was a 14-year period of massively rising government bonds starting in 1932.

In Korea, there has only been one bubble in the post-IMF era, in the form of Type 2 government housing bonds. There are still Type 1 bonds being issued under the same name, but the content is completely different.

In other words, the bonds have expired and have been fully redeemed, and the physical bonds don't even exist anymore.

At the time, apartment speculation was so intense that when applying for an apartment for sale, the highest bidder was selected as the winner by offering an estimated amount to purchase the bonds, and after winning the contract, they had to buy the government-issued Type 2 National Housing Bonds at the time of the bid to cover the amount they offered.

This system was implemented for a period of time from April 30, 1983, to curb real estate speculation in the sale of new apartments, and was abolished in 1999.

At the time, Type 2 National Housing Bonds , redeemable after 20 years, had a 5% compounded interest rate, and the bargain purchase price for collectors was around 8-9% of the face value.

A 100 million won face value Type 2 National Housing Bonds (effectively a government bond) was trading for around 9 million won. Of course, the inflation rate was over 5-6% at the time.

These bonds got the best treatment under the IMF because they were government bonds with high compound interest and were 20-year bonds that were exempt from inheritance tax. After the IMF, they were trading at a premium of 2-3 times par, so there was a huge price surge.

At 3-5% compounded interest for 20 years, the simple value calculation using the compound interest table is 81% at maturity.

At maturity, the value would have increased by more than 2,000% compared to the purchase price of 9 million won, excluding the premium. (181 million won÷9 million won)×100=2,011%, which is a return of 2,000% based on compound interest alone.

However, inflation was quite high during this period, so real estate, such as apartments, would have also seen a significant increase.

However, when the IMF situation came along and interest rates soared and government bonds were at their highest prices, real estate would have already fallen dramatically.

If you had sold the bonds when the IMF situation improved, i.e. when interest rates dropped sharply, you would have realized a profit. This shows that even the best assets need to be sold at some point, and that you shouldn't put all your money in one asset.

It's also important to note that a 10-year bond is a short-term bond if it matures in one year.It's important to note that this is based on the number of days to maturity.

Currently, there are 5, 10, 20, and 30 year government bonds traded in the secondary market, but the trading volume is not high and the amount of government bonds issued is not large, so the market is not well developed.

However, developed countries have well-developed government bond markets, and Korea will soon have the opportunity to significantly develop its government bond issuance and distribution market.

This is that time. We need to understand what the government's intention is in issuing government bonds for private investment.

Until now, taxes have been used to finance the country's management, but considering tax resistance and its relationship with economic growth, the time will soon come when government bonds will be used to finance the country like in developed countries. For this to happen, government bonds need to be speculative.

In the future, the popularity of government bonds will skyrocket, and we will see bubbles forming and trading in the government bond market.

After the current asset market bull run is over, we expect the issuance and circulation of government bonds to be greatly activated by the growing welfare demand. After that, a bubble will form in the government bond market as the deflationary economy continues.

Currently, it is still possible to trade government bonds in large quantities through ETFs, but the lack of active trading indicates that there is not much demand for government bonds yet.

A 10-year Government bond ETF doesn't actually own Government bonds, but rather bets on futures or bond yields, hedged with monetary stability bonds.

However, they can be a great way to gain from interest rate movements, so it's important to time your investments. Given that deflation is underway, this is the best place to invest. You can get the interest, and the big capital gains are on the side.

If you're looking for bigger capital gains, you should trade long-term bonds.

You can buy and sell bond ETFs when you want, in the quantities you need, and they're thought to trade at a fair price, despite some tracking error,I think. But I've already explained why physical investments are better.

Also, government bond ETFs pay 15.4% of dividend income in taxes, not to mention capital gains taxes on gains. Of course, capital gains tax on the gains will also be due next year under the name of financial investment income tax.

Chapter 17) Income Tax on Financial Investments and Investing in Government Bonds

The Financial Investment Income Tax (a tax on capital gains related to financial investments), which will be implemented from 2025, is a tax of 22 to 27.5% on capital gains over 50 million won for stock transfers and 2.5 million won for bond transfers, and will be implemented from 2025.

It should be renamed 'Financial Asset Capital Gains Tax' to avoid confusion. For each financial asset, all gains and losses will be aggregated and taxed together.

So, for example
If you make a large profit on a government bond, you'll pay a large tax. The introduction of a financial investment income tax system could cause capital to flow out of the country, and it could also be a policy that encourages short-term investments.

However, since investing under the Pentagon Investment Method requires investors to rotate through stocks, apartments, dollar swaps, savings, and government bonds in an asset-cycle sequence, long-term investments will be much less likely to be made for these reasons.

If you've been told by your stock market guru that investing in stocks for the long term will make you rich, you're in for a surprise - it won't.

With the implementation of the financial investment income tax, there may be a partial shift of funds from financial assets to real estate.

In addition, there will be cases where tax brackets will change and taxes will increase dramatically, so paying taxes and saving money will increasingly be in the hands of experts.

Since few individual investors make more than $50 million a year, this may not be as shocking as you think. It may seem that the wealthy are the most affected, but it is a fair taxation system.

This will make investing in government bonds a little less attractive, as capital gains (i.e., gains on the sale of bonds) and interest income will be subject to the financial investment income tax.

This system will make government bonds considerably less attractive as an investment, because now the capital gains tax will also apply to capital gains on the sale of bonds.

This doesn't mean that you shouldn't invest in stocks and bonds just because you're afraid of the financial investment income tax.

Investors shouldn't blindly invest in foreign stocks and bonds or in real estate, because you can't grow your wealth if you don't invest anywhere.

Until 2029 or so, when Korea's long term deflation is cured, Korean investors are strongly advised not to invest overseas, as their money will become a ghost dollar that will never return to Korea.

Japan is a very powerful counterfactual teacher for Korea, at least when it comes to the phenomenon of long term deflation and how to invest.

Epilogue

In this book, we'll take a detailed look at why and how the five most popular assets to invest in – stocks, apartments, dollars, deposits, and government bonds – crash at least once every decade, in any country and in any era, including the government bond market.

In fact, until now, there hasn't been a proper financial book on bond investing, which is something I've always been curious about.

The author is pleased to have had the opportunity to review and summarize all of the bits and pieces of bond investment knowledge that I have had so far.

This is a great opportunity to look at the fate of the largest and most prolific U.S. government bonds in history, and the great collapse of bonds, especially government bonds, due to the surge in U.S. interest rates.

It is also a great opportunity to look at the long-term surge in government bonds of other countries after the long term deflation.

Other People's Crises Are Your Opportunity for the Prepared Person. It's a commonplace truth that great riches are born in times of crisis

The author examines government bond investments in general, including the case of Korea. In fact, this book summarizes the general theory of government bond investments, tips for making big money, and the general theory of government bond investments as a hedge against risk.

In other words, these facts can occur in any country at any time. Therefore, it is a general theory of government bond investing that can always be applied.

In fact, when people, especially government officials, formulate policies, they often analyze overseas examples to introduce or improve new systems.

This book analyzes in detail the economic development policies of South Korea as a developing country, including how it used government bonds to move from being one of the poorest countries to becoming a developed country.

Until now, investing in government bonds has been the exclusive realm of big money managers. Now, as the Pentagon Investment Method summarizes tips for investing in government bonds, it is important to remember that government bonds are the last investment option in the five stages of the asset cycle of stocks, apartments, dollars, deposits, and government bonds.

In other words, it is an investment asset that you must go through at least once in your 10-year financial life. Right now, the world is in a long period of deflation, except for Japan.

Sometimes people ask the me what is the basis of the book, but I mainly presents the data of the FRB as the evidence in the book.

I do not rely on the theories of any theorist. It is all original, meaning that I do not quote any other theories or books.

Since this is the first book on bond bubbles, specifically the collapse of the government bond bubble, there are no other books on the market to reference.

Since I wrote the first book on the collapse of the government bond bubble, there is no book out there to quote from. I can only refer back to books that have already been published.

It has been 40 years since the author has been studying and investing in financial technology in earnest. My grandsons, Siyoon Kim and Hyunbae Sohn, are already in middle school and elementary school.

It's the age of shorts on YouTube. You have to keep it short and to the point to get readers to read. This is the secret to getting rich investing in government bonds: especially government bonds, in a long term deflation, is a complete jackpot.

If you do the opposite and invest in government bonds, you will be completely destroying your wealth. The age of hyper-polarization of wealth is upon us.

With long-term deflation in full swing and nowhere to invest, deflation is not the scariest thing, but the ultra-long-term rally in government bond prices is.

In Japan, interest rates were negative for a long time. In this case, the rest of the world, including Korea, will see interest rates fall to near negative rates, just as Japan did in the past.

While Japan has survived 32 years of long term deflation, the rest of the world is now in the midst of long term deflation.

The subprime financial crisis and the coronavirus pandemic have triggered inflation due to the largest amount of dollar money ever released.

However, the current inflation is a pause on the way to long term deflation. There is also a new variable. If Trump is re-elected in the U.S. presidential election, he is likely to impose additional tariffs on Chinese goods as a further check on China. This could lead to a longer inflationary period.

He is also expected to raise tariffs even on friendly countries. If this happens, we can expect a further hike in the US interest rate to curb inflation.

Eventually, inflation and US interest rates could move into a Higher for Longer state. For a longer period of time, this could be the normal state.

However, the fact that we are in the midst of a long term deflation around the world is also a fact. It's a time of chaos, but the tips I've summarized for investing in bonds (government bonds) don't change just because the time frame has slowed down.

If you can cope with the fluctuations in interest rates, you will always succeed in investing in government bonds. Finally, I emphasize once again that you shouldn't invest in any bonds other than government bonds.

I hope that all readers will take advantage of this opportunity to invest in government bonds exclusively and make a lot of money. I end this book with the hope that you will be able to say "Life is beautiful!" when you are old.

2024.6.2
by Sohn daeshig